THE PUFFIN REFERENCE ATLAS OF THE WORLD

PUFFIN BOOKS

Puffin Books, Penguin Books Ltd, Harmondsworth, Middlesex, England
Viking Penguin Inc., 40 West 23rd Street, New York, New York 10010, U.S.A.
Penguin Books Australia Ltd, Ringwood, Victoria, Australia
Penguin Books Canada Limited, 2801 John Street, Markham, Ontario, Canada L3R 1B4
Penguin Books (N.Z.) Ltd, 182—190 Wairau Road, Auckland 10, New Zealand

First published by John Bartholomew & Son Limited, 1985
as *The Illustrated Reference Atlas of the World*
Published in Puffin Books 1986

Made and printed in Great Britain by John Bartholomew & Son Ltd
Typeset in Times

Cover photograph courtesy of NASA

Acknowledgements

The Publishers acknowledge with thanks the assistance of the following in preparing this publication:
Dr Walter Stephen
Senior Adviser, Curriculum, Dean Education Centre, Edinburgh
Alister Hendrie
Assistant Headteacher, Portobello High School, Edinburgh
Andrew Grant
Principal Teacher, Geography, Wester Hailes Education Centre, Edinburgh
Stephen Hamilton
Principal Teacher, Geography, Broughton High School, Edinburgh

The Publishers are grateful to the following for providing the photographs used in this atlas:
(picture number(s) shown in italics)
Travel Photo International: pages 6-7, savanna, rain forest, prairie, northern forest; page 12, *7*; page 21, *2*; page 27, *11*; page 28, *4*, *5*, *13*, *14*; page 30, *7*; page 31, *2*; page 46, *3*, *4*; page 54, *3*, *4*
Photographers' Library: pages 6-7, scrub *Chris Knaggs photograph*, desert *Oliver Martel photograph* page 10, *8 Clive Sawyer photograph*; page 26, *8 Ian Wright photograph* page 29, *9 Tom Hustler photograph*; page 30, *4 Robyn Beeche photograph*
Biofotos page 10, *5 Heather Angel photograph*; page 30, *6 Andrew Henley photograph* page 31, *3 Soames Summerhays photograph*
The Photo Source page 12, *10*; page 21, *4*; page 26, *7*
Wade Cooper Associates, Edinburgh page 28, *12*; page 29, *10*; page 46, *1*
Pictor International page 26, *6*; page 46, *2*
B. and C. Alexander pages 6-7, tundra
Bruce Coleman Ltd page 54, *6 WWF/Eugen Schuhmacher photograph*
Mepha page 21, *1 C. Osborne photograph*
Michael Scott pages 6-7, woodland and grass
Yorkshire and Humberside Tourist Board page 11, *2*

CONTENTS

INTRODUCTION

This atlas for the 8-13 age group bridges the gap between pictorial atlases intended for young children and the much more complex atlases published for adults. The political and physical maps are just like those in a 'proper' atlas, drawn to scale with layer colouring to show how high the land is. But they have been simplified to make it easy to find country names, borders, main towns and physical features such as rivers and mountains. Where there is an English version of a place name, it is given first followed by the local language version.

The layout of the atlas is easy to follow. Pages 4 and 5 show how flat, two-dimensional maps can be drawn to show the rounded, three-dimensional world, and explain the idea of scale as it relates to maps. The map of world environments on pages 6 and 7 shows the 8 different climatic areas found in the world, with descriptions of the types of vegetation to be seen in each area. The key map and key to symbols on pages 8 and 9 will help in understanding and using the maps. Each of the boxes on the key map outlines an area covered by a particular map in the atlas. The number of the page where the map can be found is given in the inside top right-hand corner of each box. The symbols used on the maps are also explained, with examples.

The main part of the atlas, pages 10-58, is divided into continental sections – Europe, Africa, etc. Each section begins with a political map naming the countries included. Gazetteers for some of the larger countries show their flags and list their size, population, capital, language and currency. A 'Did you know that?' panel gives details of more unusual and surprising facts and places, some of which are illustrated. All the facts are keyed with numbers to their location on the political map. The number of each fact, the number of its picture (if there is one) and its number on the map are all the same. E.g. Fact ❹ is illustrated in picture ❹ and ❹ on the map shows where in the world it can be found. There are also maps showing population distribution, and the type of natural vegetation and products of each part of the continent. A location globe shows exactly where the area covered in the political map is, in relation to the rest of the world. Physical maps covering each part of the continent in more detail make up the rest of the continental section. On every map spread there is another location globe which provides a quick answer to the question 'Where in the world is that?'.

The last six pages of the atlas contain an index to many of the places and geographical features shown on the maps. Each entry gives the name of the place, what it is (island, region etc), the name of the country or part of the world where it can be found, and a page number and grid reference. So the entry: London *Eng* **16C3**, refers to London, England which can be found on the map on page 16, in the area located by running a finger down from the letter C at the top of the page and in from the number 3 at the side of the page.

SCALE

Scale means how big one thing is, compared to another. For example, a model car can be a scale model of a real car. Drawing something 'to scale' is a way of making a picture or map of something big fit on to a small piece of paper. The important fact about a scale model or scale drawing is that from it, you can find out the size of the real thing – whether it is a car or a country. All you need to know is the scale that was used. The scale of a scale drawing will be shown on the scale bar beside it. It might look like this:

0 1 2 3 4 5m

A short length (for example 1 cm) on the scale bar will stand for a longer one (for example 1 m) in the real world. By measuring the drawing and converting your measurements using the scale bar, you know the size of the real thing.

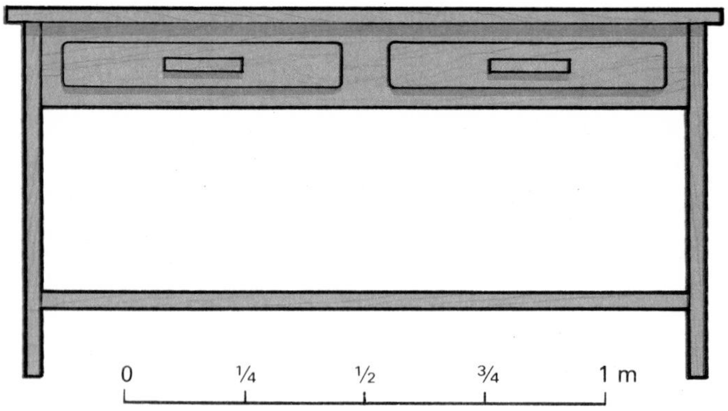

The picture shows a scale drawing of a table. Measure it to find out how long and high the real table was (use the scale bar!).

As you make scale drawings of bigger and bigger things, the short length on the scale bar has to stand for longer and longer lengths in the real world. Otherwise the drawings would not fit on to pieces of paper that could be held easily. Look at the plan of the classroom. What scale is it drawn to? How long are the walls of the real classroom?

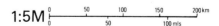

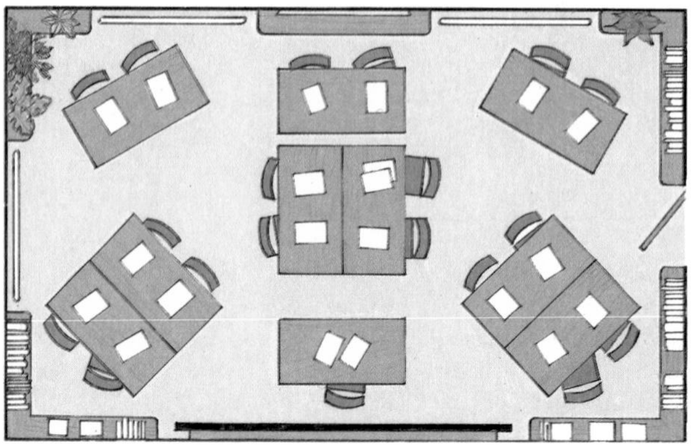

0 1 2 3 4 m

Cartographers (people who draw maps) make scale drawings of very big things – places and countries. So a small length on a map (for example 1 cm) has to stand for a very large one in real life (for example 1 km (100 000 cm) or 50 km (5 000 000 cm)). These examples could be written 1:100 000 or 1:5M (M stands for 'million'). When a scale is written like this, it is called a Representative Fraction (RF for short). Most maps have a scale bar as well as an RF. So if two places on a map are 6 cm apart and at the top of the page you see this:

1:5M 0 50 100 150 200 km / 0 50 100 mls

you can work out that the real places are 300 km apart.

All the maps in this atlas have an RF and scale bar at the top of the page. The scale of the maps varies, depending on the size of the area each has to show.

MAP PROJECTIONS

People who make flat maps have one big problem: the world is spherical (like an orange). If you peel the skin off an orange

you will discover that you cannot make the pieces of skin lie flat unless you push them out of shape. In the same way, if map makers want to draw a flat map, they have to change the shapes or sizes (or both) of the countries on the surface of the earth. The only kind of map without these distortions (as the changes in shape and size are called) is a globe – a spherical map (right).

Over the centuries, many different ways of making flat maps of the earth have been discovered. They are called **Map Projections**. A projector makes an image on a screen by shining a light through a piece of film. Map makers pretended to shine a light through from the inside of the world and drew the outlines of countries as they would look on a flat surface. This type of map is called an **Azimuthal Projection**.

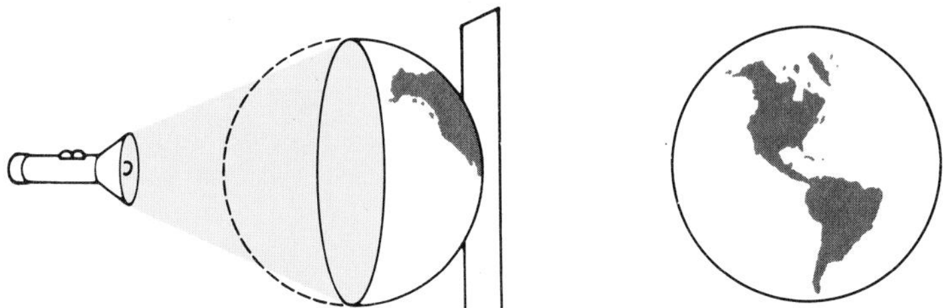

AZIMUTHAL

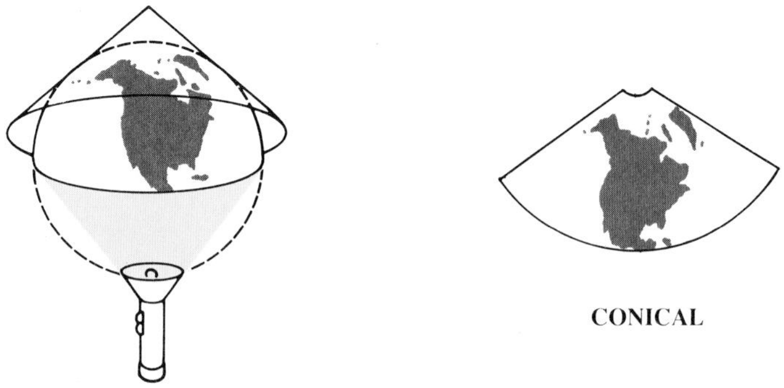

CONICAL

By 'shining a light' through different parts of the world (the top, the sides and so on) different maps could be drawn. The next step was to change the shape of the 'screen' onto which the outlines of countries were projected. Some map makers used a cone shape. Their maps are called **Conical Projections**. Others used a cylinder shape, as if a piece of paper had been wrapped round the world. A map made like this is called a **Cylindrical Projection**. Other ways of drawing maps were developed, which did not use this idea of 'shining a light', but they are all called 'projections' from the first way of drawing them.

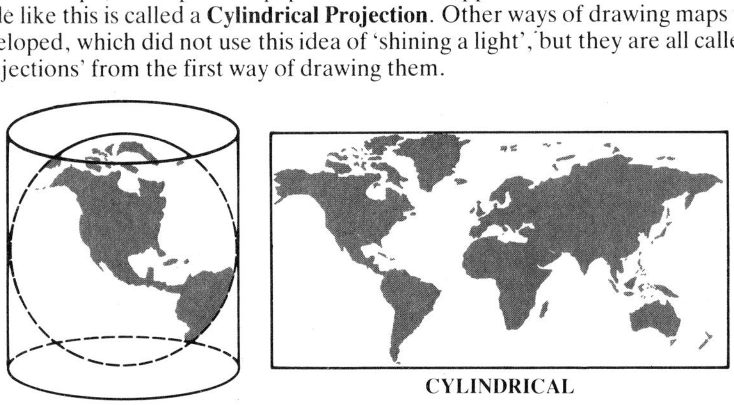

CYLINDRICAL

All projections distort land and sea areas and their positions in different ways. Map makers choose the projection they want to use depending on what the map is for. They consider things like relative sizes of areas, shapes of areas, directions and distances. Look at the box on the right, showing Australia drawn using three different projections (there are many more than that); see how different the shape of the country is.

THREE PROJECTIONS OF AUSTRALIA

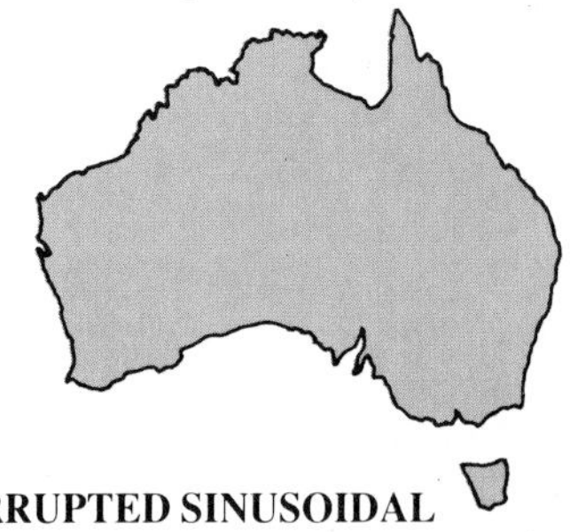

INTERRUPTED SINUSOIDAL
Distances are accurate along all parallels of latitude and on each centre meridian.

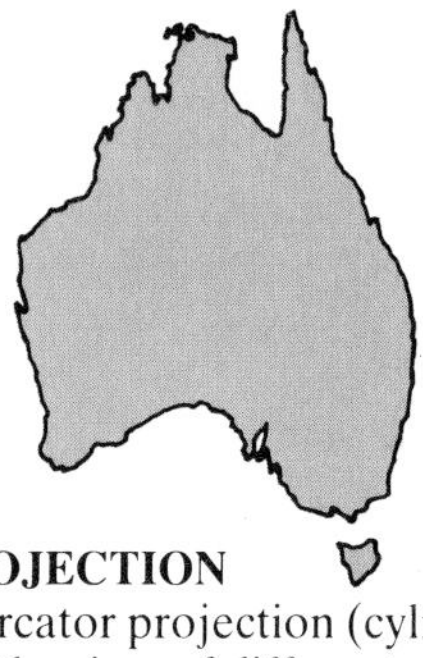

PETERS PROJECTION
Modified Mercator projection (cylindrical) which tries to show the sizes of different countries in proportion to each other. Often used for maps showing the inequality of wealth distribution in proportion to country size and population.

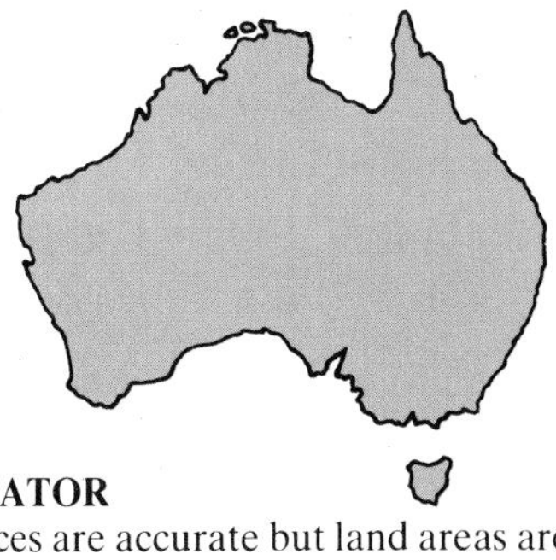

MERCATOR
Distances are accurate but land areas are distorted; traditionally used for navigation; the most popular projection in the past for world maps.

6 WORLD MAP OF THE ENVIRONMENT

The world can be divided into 8 broad 'climatic zones' (these are areas with a particular sort of weather). The natural types of plants and animals found in each zone are different and depend on the weather the zone has. This map shows which parts of the world are in each zone. The colour of the strip at the top of each zone description (for example, Desert, Rainforest) is the same as the colour used for the zone on the big map. The little map beside each zone description pinpoints where that type of habitat is found in the world. (For example, the Desert strip is orange/yellow. The little sketch map shows you where on the big map to look for this colour. You will find this colour in the north of Africa, the west of North America and in parts of Asia and Australia. All these places have deserts. The description tells you what the natural countryside looks like and what plants and animals live there.)

SCRUB OR MEDITERRANEAN

Areas of long, hot, dry summers and short, warm winters. The land used to be covered with trees, but man cleared it for crops and grazed his animals on it. Now there is evergreen scrub – vines and olive trees.

TUNDRA OR MOUNTAIN

Polar areas which are usually frozen over. During the short summers the top layer of soil thaws, creating vast marshes. Compact, wind-resistant plants and lichens and mosses are found here. Animals include lemmings and reindeer.

NORTHERN FOREST (TAIGA)

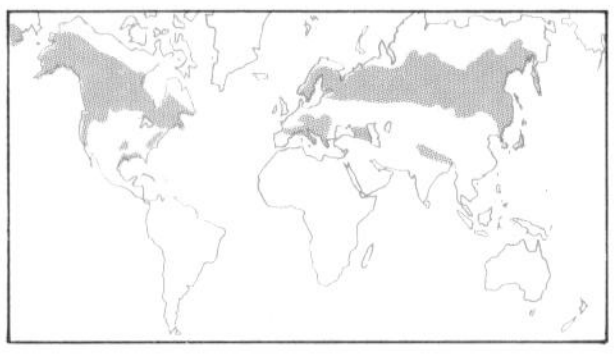

Forests of conifers growing over a large area. Winters are very cold and long. Summers are short. Trees include spruce and fir. Animals found here include beavers, squirrels and red deer.

WOODLAND AND GRASS

Temperate areas (where the weather is seldom very cold or very hot). Deciduous trees (which lose their leaves in winter) grow in the woodlands. They include oak, beech and maple. Man uses these areas most of all, for farming, building towns and villages, and industry.

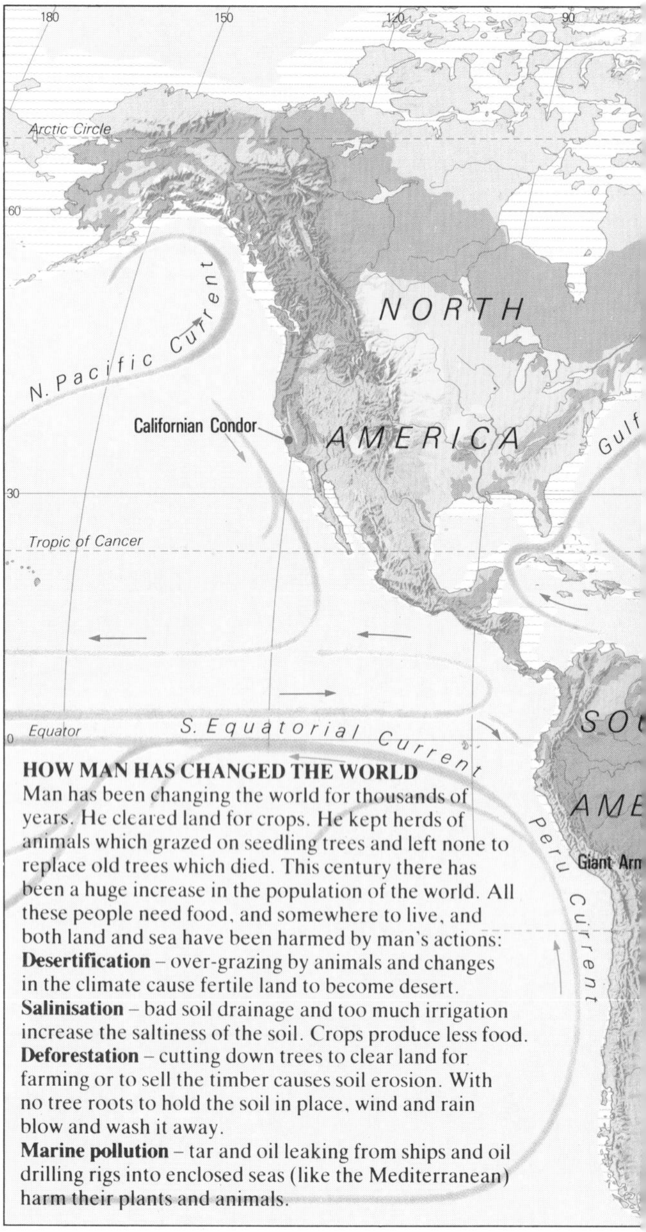

HOW MAN HAS CHANGED THE WORLD

Man has been changing the world for thousands of years. He cleared land for crops. He kept herds of animals which grazed on seedling trees and left none to replace old trees which died. This century there has been a huge increase in the population of the world. All these people need food, and somewhere to live, and both land and sea have been harmed by man's actions:

Desertification – over-grazing by animals and changes in the climate cause fertile land to become desert.

Salinisation – bad soil drainage and too much irrigation increase the saltiness of the soil. Crops produce less food.

Deforestation – cutting down trees to clear land for farming or to sell the timber causes soil erosion. With no tree roots to hold the soil in place, wind and rain blow and wash it away.

Marine pollution – tar and oil leaking from ships and oil drilling rigs into enclosed seas (like the Mediterranean) harm their plants and animals.

GRASSLAND

Hot summers, cold winters and moderate rainfall. Huge area of grassland and 'black' (very fertile) soils. Grain crops grow well, and so does rich pasture for beef cattle. Names for this kind of grassland include steppe, veld, pampas and prairie.

SAVANNA

Tall grasses with thick stems, and flat-topped thorny trees grow here. Animals grazing here include giraffes and zebras. There is a short rainy season. Often it does not rain for a long time (a drought). Fires burn the dried out plants but they have adapted to survive this and grow again.

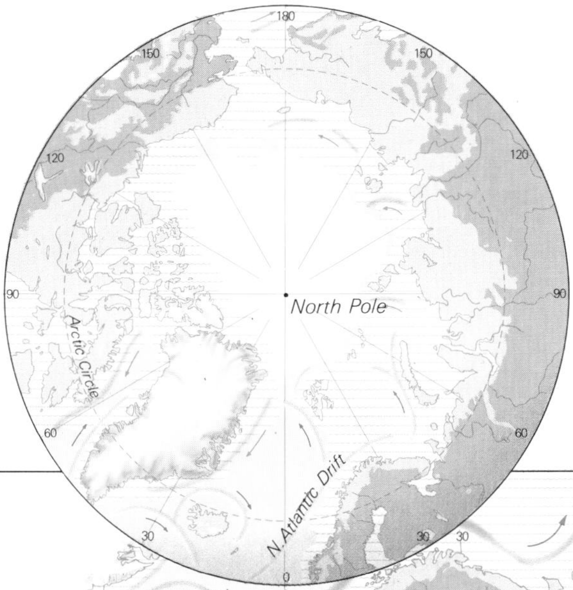

DESERT

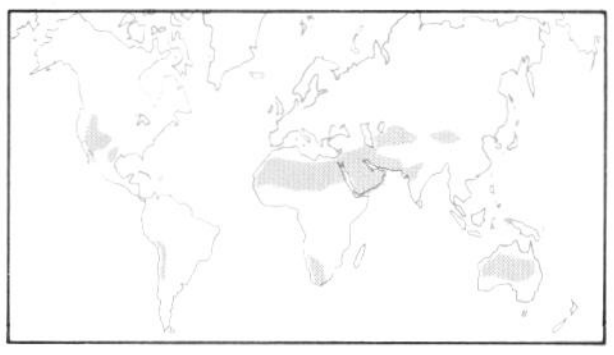

These areas have bare mountains, rocky wastes and sand dunes. Plants (wiry grass, thorn bushes and cacti) and animals (lizards and camels) must be well adapted to survive very high temperatures and little water. It may rain only once in several years.

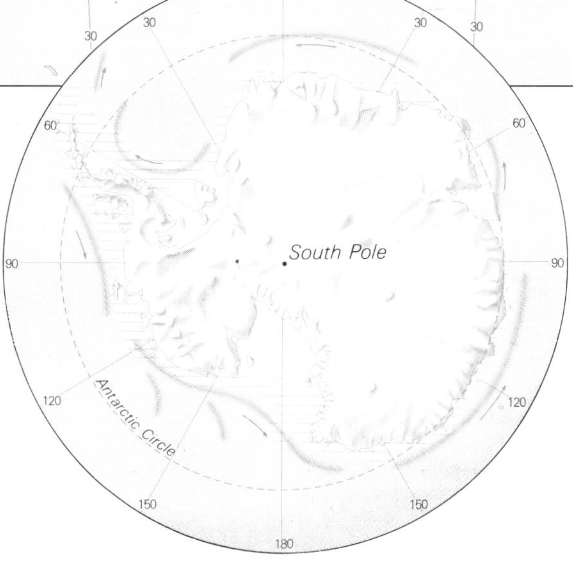

RAINFOREST

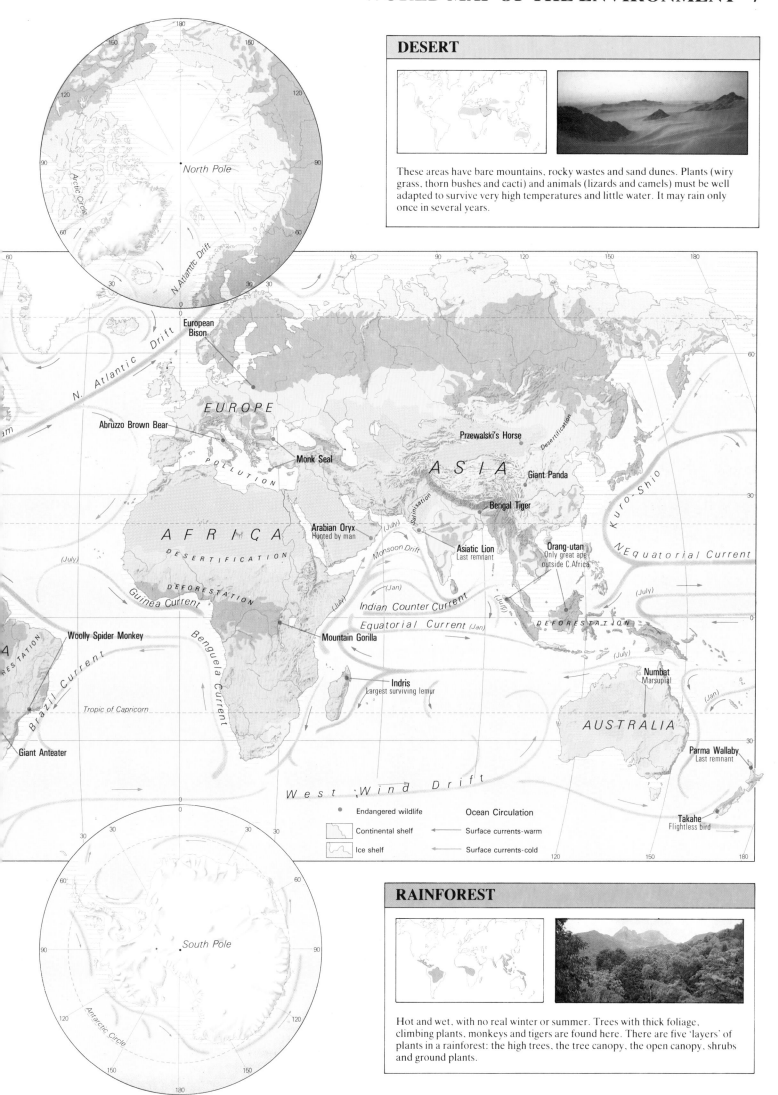

Hot and wet, with no real winter or summer. Trees with thick foliage, climbing plants, monkeys and tigers are found here. There are five 'layers' of plants in a rainforest: the high trees, the tree canopy, the open canopy, shrubs and ground plants.

8 KEY MAP

This map shows you which part of the world is shown in each of the regional maps in this atlas. The area of each regional map is outlined in black (physical maps) or red (political maps). In the top right hand corner of each map box is a number (or two numbers) e.g. 16, 38-39. This is the number of the page or pages where you will find a map of the area within the black, or red-outlined box. The list below gives the name of each map.

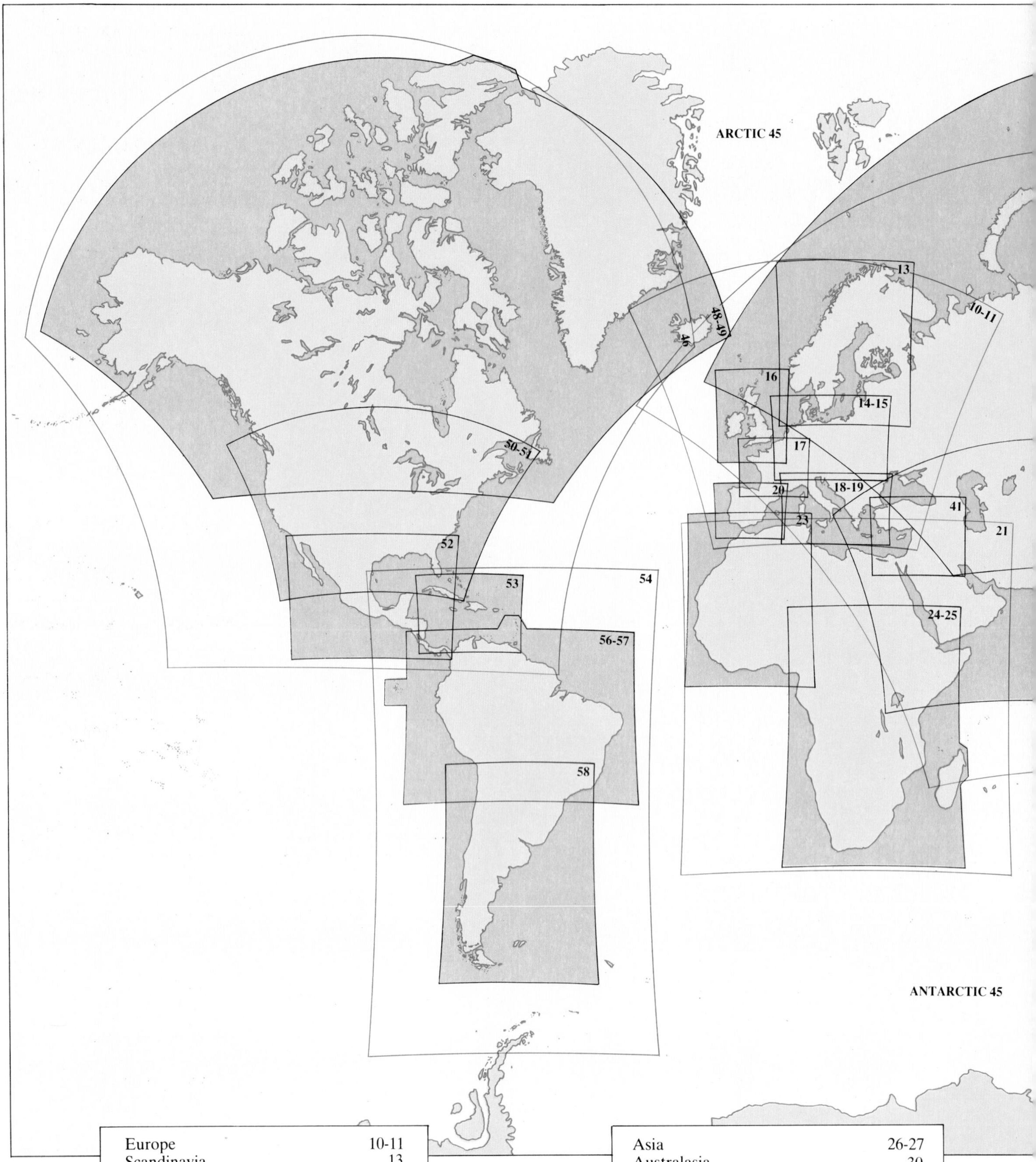
ARCTIC 45
13
10-11
48-49
46
16
14-15
17
18-19
20
23
41
21
50-51
52
53
54
56-57
24-25
58
ANTARCTIC 45

Europe	10-11
Scandinavia	13
North Central Europe	14-15
Great Britain and Ireland	16
France	17
Italy and the Balkans	18-19
Spain and Portugal	20
Africa	21
Africa West	23
Africa Central and South	24-25

Asia	26-27
Australasia	30
Union of Soviet Socialist Republics	32-33
Far East	34-35
Central China	36
Japan and Korea	37
South Asia and Middle East	38-39
South East Asia	40
Turkey, Syria and Iraq	41
Australia and South West Pacific	42-43
New Zealand	44
Polar Regions	45

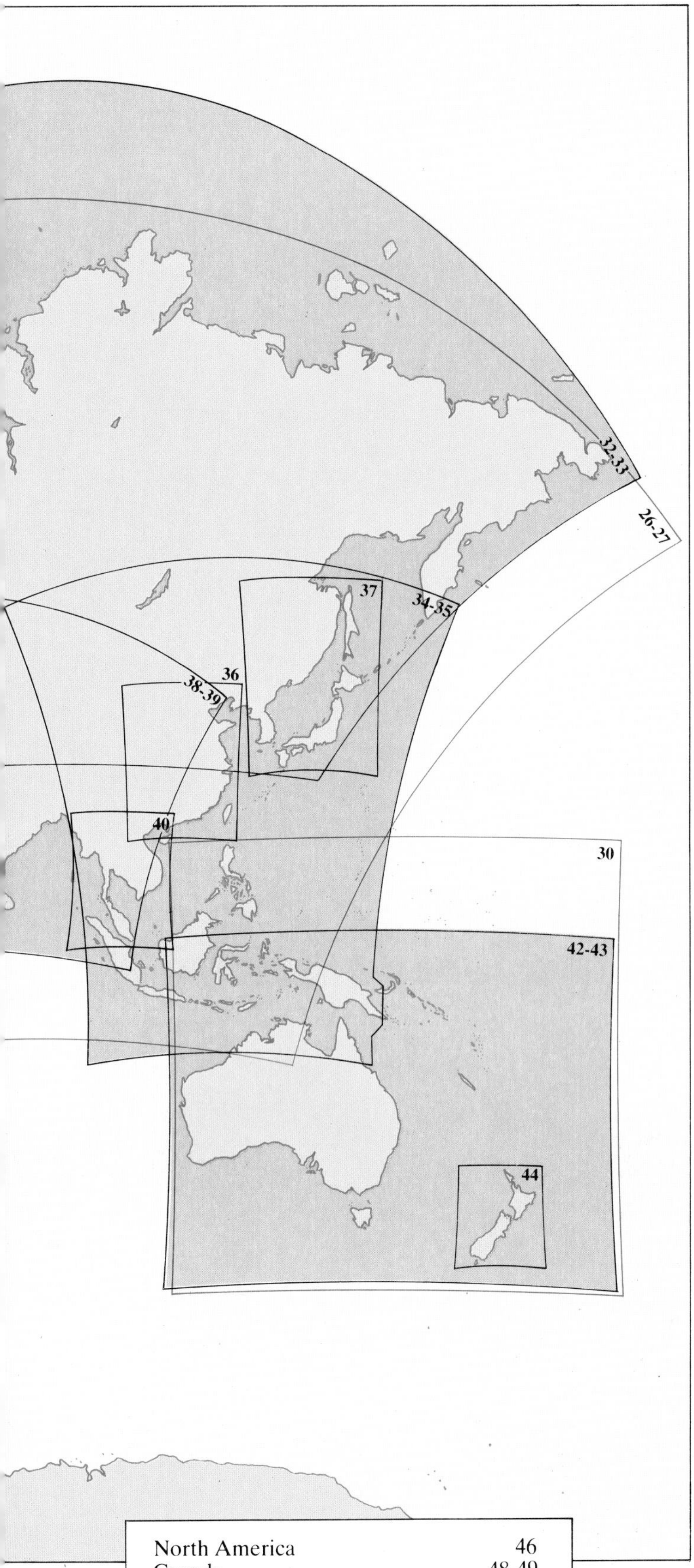

This panel explains the different lettering styles, the main symbols and the height and depth colours used on the reference maps in this atlas.

LETTERING STYLES

CANADA	Independent Nation
FLORIDA	State, Province or Autonomous Region
Gibraltar (U.K.)	Sovereignty of Dependent Territory
Lothian	Administrative Area
LANGUEDOC	Historic Region
Loire *Vosges*	Physical Feature or Physical Region

TOWNS AND CITIES

Square symbols mark capital cities — *Population*

New York	over 5 000 000
Montréal	over 1 000 000
Ottawa	over 500 000
Québec	over 100 000
St John's	over 50 000

Built-up-area

BOUNDARIES

International

International under Dispute

Cease Fire Line

Autonomous or State

Administrative

Maritime (National)

International Date Line

LANDSCAPE FEATURES

Glacier, Ice Cap

Marsh, Swamp

Sand Desert, Dunes

LAKE FEATURES

Freshwater

Saltwater

Seasonal

Salt Pan

OTHER FEATURES

River

Seasonal River

Pass, Gorge

Dam, Barrage

Waterfall, Rapid

Aqueduct

Reef

▲4231 Summit, Peak

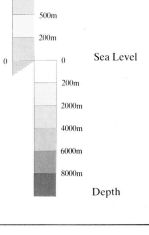

Height

6000m
5000m
4000m
3000m
2000m
1000m
500m
200m
0 — 0 Sea Level
200m
2000m
4000m
6000m
8000m

Depth

1:15M

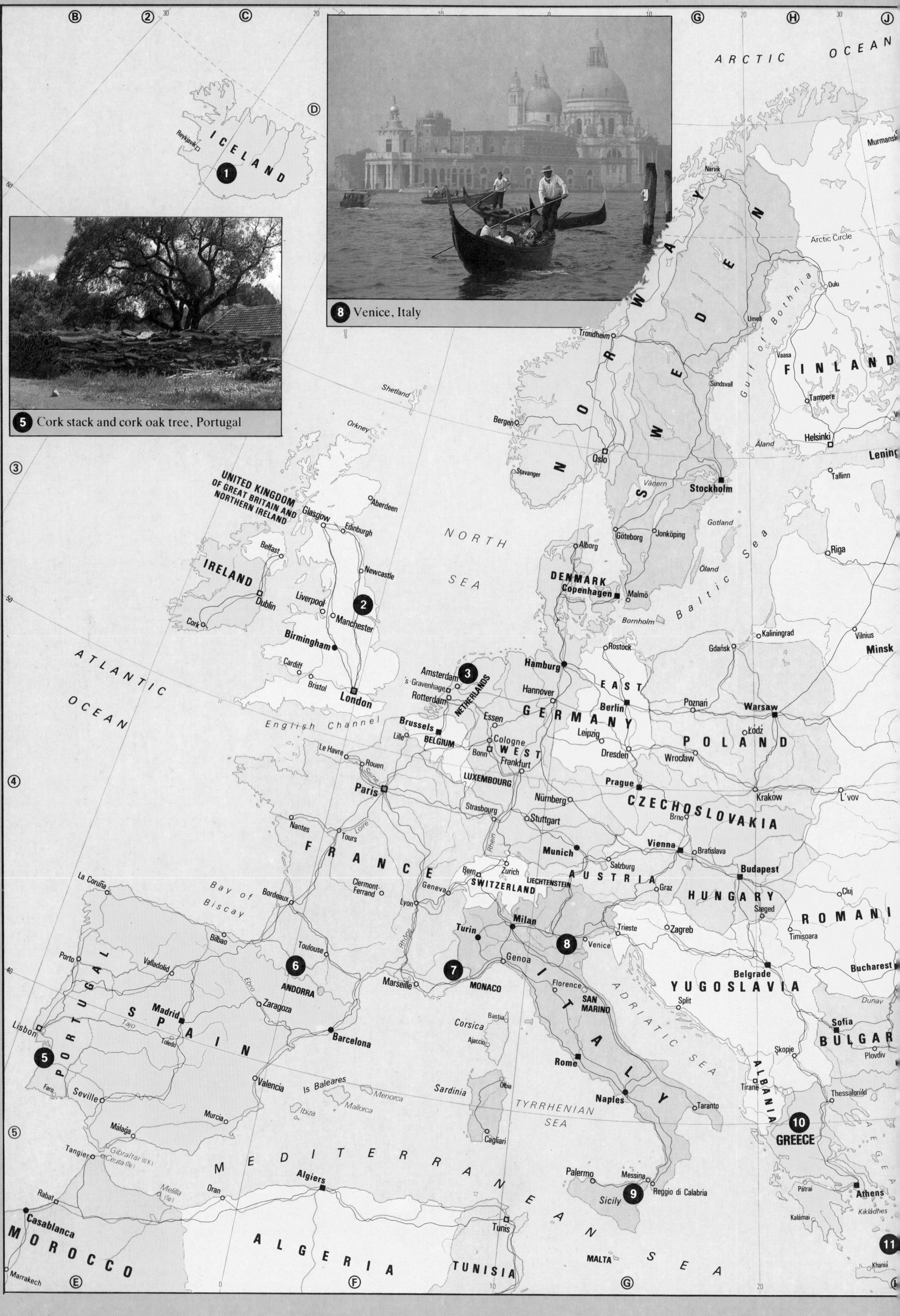

5 Cork stack and cork oak tree, Portugal

8 Venice, Italy

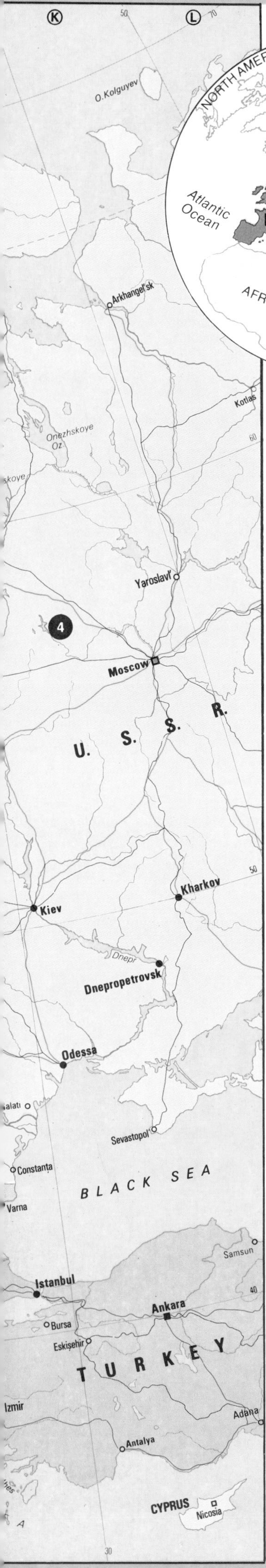

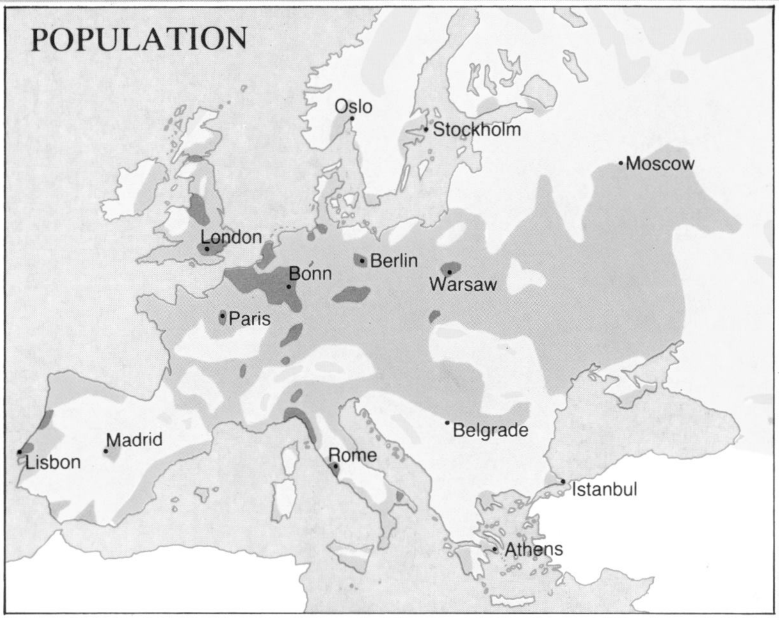

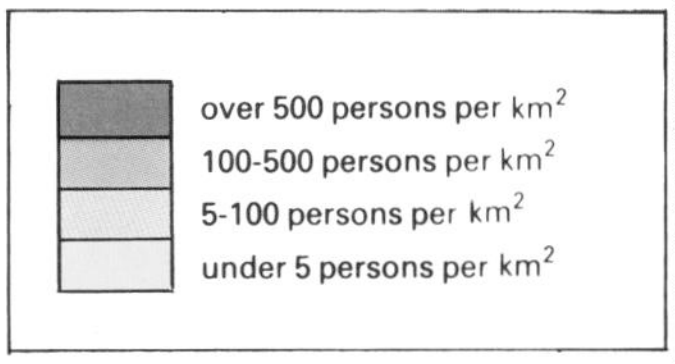

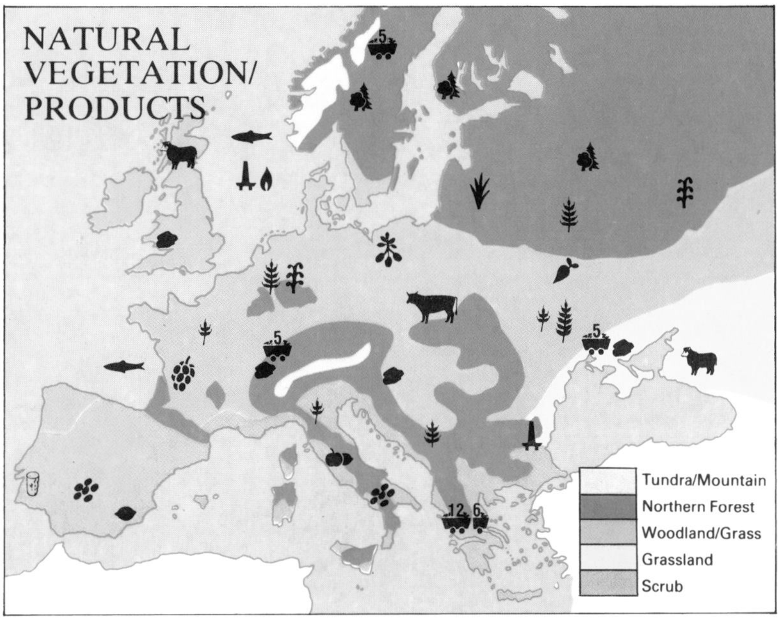

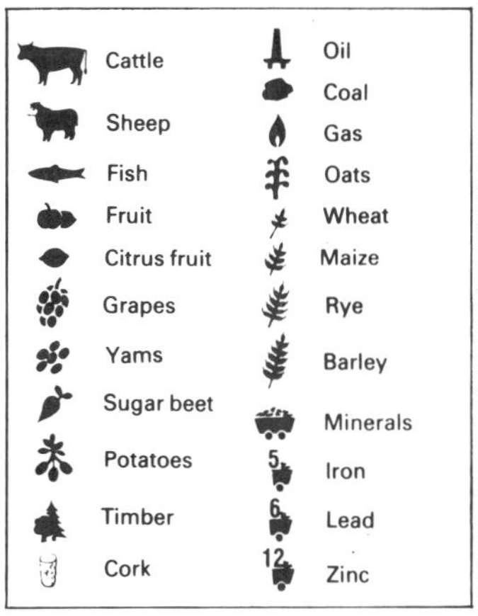

DID YOU KNOW THAT ...?

1 In Iceland, ice and fire exist side by side! Many active volcanoes and geysers (hot springs which shoot a column of water into the air at intervals) can be seen, while glaciers (continually moving 'rivers' of ice) and ice sheets cover much of the land. One volcano – Vatnajokull – is particularly dangerous for an unusual reason: it is underneath a glacier and when it erupts, the ice melts very quickly, causing terrible floods.

2 The Humber Bridge, England, has the longest main span of any bridge in the world. It stretches for 1410 m (4626 feet).

3 More than a third of the land area of the Netherlands has been reclaimed from the sea! These lands (the *polders*) are below sea level and the sea is kept out by dykes. Drainage ditches divide the fertile fields. The water from them is pumped into canals and rivers, then out to sea.

4 The longest river in Europe is the Volga, which runs for 3690 km (2293 miles) from the forests north west of Moscow all the way to the Caspian Sea.

5 Portugal is an important source of cork, which is actually the bark of a tree! The cork oak produces cork bark up to 15 cm (6 inches) thick and this is stripped off the trees every 10 to 15 years. Cork oaks grow throughout the western and central Mediterranean region.

6 The Pierre Saint Martin Cavern in the Pyrenees mountains, France, is the deepest cave system yet discovered in the world. It goes 1330 m (4364 feet) into the heart of the mountains.

7 The principality of Monaco is one of the most crowded countries in the world: 28 000 people live on 1.9 sq km (467 acres) of land! By contrast, most of Scandinavia has fewer than 40 people per square kilometre!

8 Venice, Italy, is built on no less than 118 islands! Instead of roads, there are canals, and boats are used for transport. Venice is sinking at a rate of 12 inches each century. Some of the reasons for this include water being extracted from wells, and the compression of the mud on the floor of the lagoon.

9 Mount Etna, Sicily, is the highest volcano in Europe (about 3323 m, 10 902 ft) and is still very active. Despite this, many people live on its lower slopes! This is because the soil there is very fertile and grows good produce.

2 The Humber Bridge, England

AUSTRIA

Area: 83 848 sq km
(32 374 sq miles)
Population: 7 600 000
Capital: Vienna
Language: German
Currency: Schilling

BELGIUM

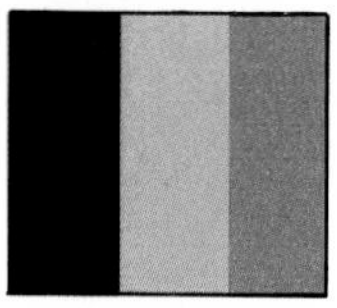

Area: 30 512 sq km
(11 781 sq miles)
Population: 9 900 000
Capital: Brussels
Languages: Flemish, French
Currency: Belgian Franc

DENMARK

Area: 43 030 sq km
(16 614 sq miles)
Population: 5 100 000
Capital: Copenhagen
Language: Danish
Currency: Krone

EAST GERMANY

Area: 107 860 sq km
(41 645 miles)
Population: 16 700 000
Capital: Berlin (East)
Language: German
Currency: DDR Mark

FRANCE

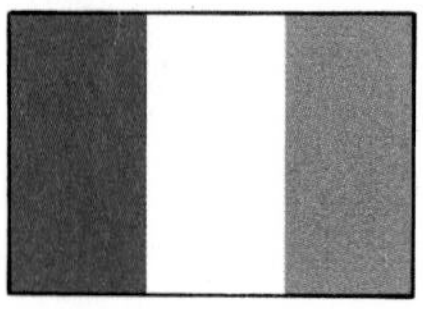

Area: 551 000 sq km
(212 741 sq miles)
Population: 54 800 000
Capital: Paris
Language: French
Currency: Franc

GREECE

Area: 131 955 sq km
(50 948 sq miles)
Population: 10 000 000
Capital: Athens
Language: Greek
Currency: Drachma

IRELAND

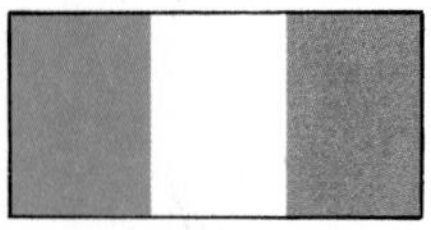

Area: 70 282 sq km
(27 136 sq miles)
Population: 3 600 000
Capital: Dublin
Languages: Irish (Gaelic), English
Currency: Irish Pound (Punt)

ITALY

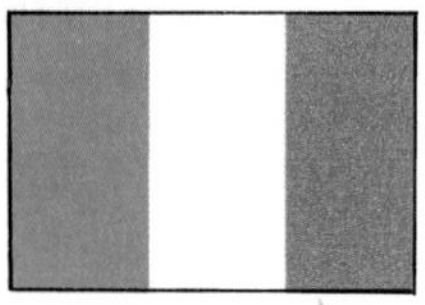

Area: 301 245 sq km
(116 311 sq miles)
Population: 57 000 000
Capital: Rome
Language: Italian
Currency: Lira

NETHERLANDS

Area: 33 940 sq km
(13 104 sq miles)
Population: 14 400 000
Capital: The Hague
Language: Dutch
Currency: Guilder

POLAND

Area: 312 683 sq km
(120 727 sq miles)
Population: 36 900 000
Capital: Warsaw
Language: Polish
Currency: Zloty

PORTUGAL

Area: 91 671 sq km
(35 394 sq miles)
Population: 10 100 000
Capital: Lisbon
Language: Portuguese
Currency: Escudo

SPAIN

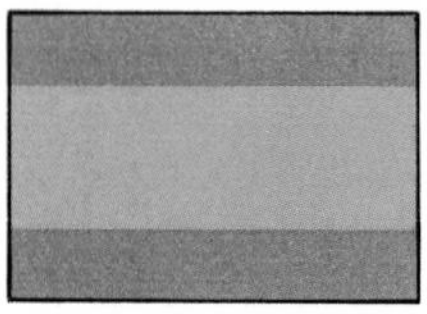

Area: 504 745 sq km
(194 882 sq miles)
Population: 38 400 000
Capital: Madrid
Language: Spanish
Currency: Peseta

UNITED KINGDOM

Area: 244 104 sq km
(94 249 sq miles)
Population: 56 000 000
Capital: London
Language: English
Currency: Pound Sterling

WEST GERMANY

Area: 248 528 sq km
(95 957 sq miles)
Population: 61 400 000
Capital: Bonn
Language: German
Currency: Deutschmark

YUGOSLAVIA

Area: 255 803 sq km
(98 766 sq miles)
Population: 23 000 000
Capital: Belgrade
Languages: Serbo-Croatian, Macedonian, Slovenian
Currency: Dinar

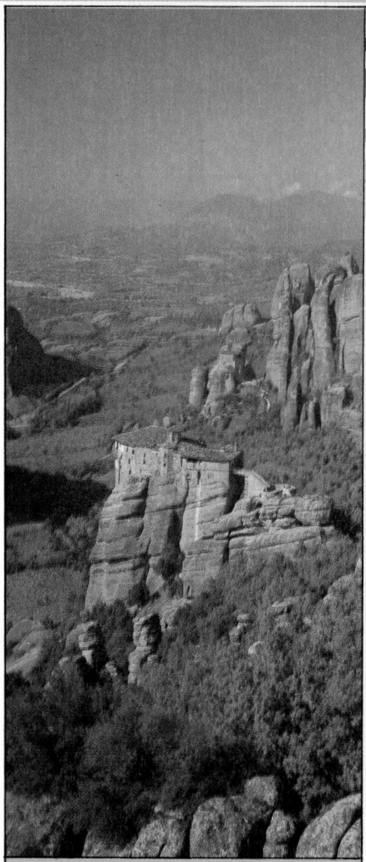

10 Monasteries on rock pillars, Greece

10 Near Kalabaka, Greece, are a group of monasteries built for monks with no fear of heights! They are perched on top of pillars of rock, called meteora, 300 m (1 000 ft) high! The only way up was by ladders or baskets slung on the end of ropes. Now stairways have been constructed so that tourists can visit the buildings.

11 The island of Santorini (Thira) in Greece is the site of the world's largest natural disaster. About 1500 BC this volcanic island erupted leaving a *caldera* (hollow basin shape where the top of the volcano had been) about 13 km (8 miles) across. Many people believe that the destruction of this island is the origin of the story of Atlantis. The people of Atlantis are mentioned by the Greek writer Plato. Crime and corruption spread throughout their island as they became wealthier, until finally the Athenians conquered them. Later the island disappeared into the sea in a single day and night.

7 Monte Carlo, Monaco

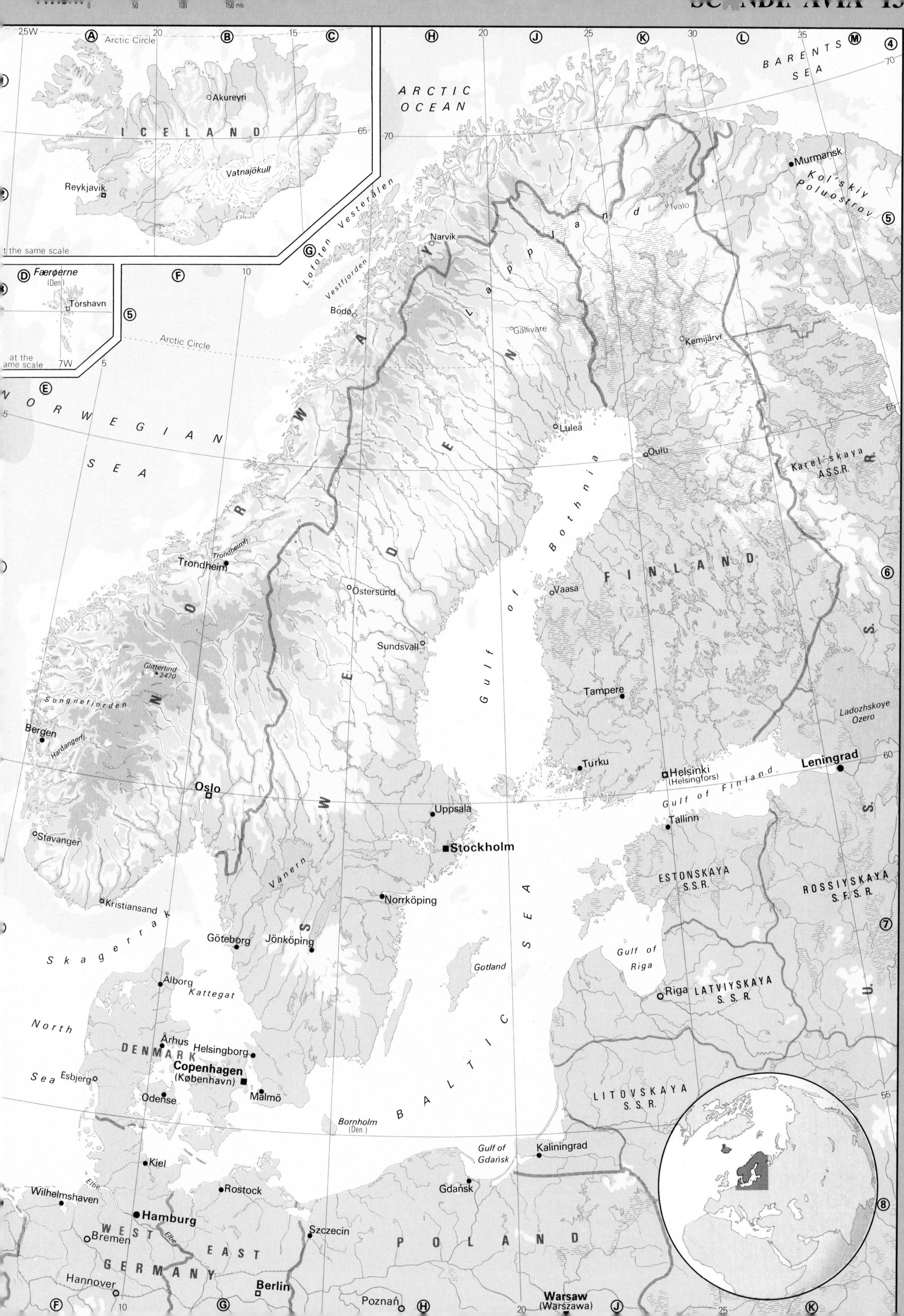
0 50 100 150 mls
25W
A
B
C
20
15
Arctic Circle
Akureyri
ICELAND
65
Vatnajökull
Reykjavik
at the same scale
D
Færøerne
(Den.)
Torshavn
at the
same scale
7W
E
F
5
10
Arctic Circle
H
J
K
L
M
4
5
6
7
8
20
25
30
35
70
65
60
55
ARCTIC
OCEAN
BARENTS
SEA
Murmansk
Kol'skiy
Poluostrov
Ivalo
Lappland
Narvik
Lofoten Vesterålen
G
Vestfjorden
Bodø
Gällivare
Kemijärvi
NORWEGIAN
SEA
NORWAY
SWEDEN
Luleå
Oulu
Karel'skaya
A.S.S.R.
Gulf of Bothnia
Trondheimfj.
Trondheim
Östersund
Vaasa
FINLAND
Sundsvall
Glittertind
2470
Songnefjorden
Bergen
Hardangerfj.
Tampere
Ladozhskoye
Ozero
Turku
Helsinki
(Helsingfors)
Leningrad
Gulf of Finland
Oslo
Uppsala
Stavanger
Stockholm
Tallinn
U.S.S.R.
Vänern
ESTONSKAYA
S.S.R.
ROSSIYSKAYA
S.F.S.R.
Kristiansand
Norrköping
Skagerrak
Göteborg
Jönköping
Gotland
Gulf of
Riga
Ålborg
Kattegat
Riga
LATVIYSKAYA
S. S. R.
North
Sea
BALTIC SEA
DENMARK
Århus
Helsingborg
Copenhagen
(København)
Esbjerg
Odense
Malmö
LITOVSKAYA
S. S. R.
Bornholm
(Den.)
Gulf of
Gdańsk
Kaliningrad
Kiel
Rostock
Gdańsk
Elbe
Wilhelmshaven
Hamburg
WEST
GERMANY
EAST
Elbe
Bremen
Szczecin
POLAND
Hannover
Berlin
Poznań
Warsaw
(Warszawa)
F
G
H
J
K

Göteborg
Jönköping
Ålborg
Kattegat
SWEDEN
DENMARK
Århus
Jutland (Jylland)
Esbjerg
Odense
Fyn
Sjælland
Copenhagen (København)
Helsingborg
Malmö
Lolland
BALT
NORTH SEA
SCHLESWIG-HOLSTEIN
Elbe
Hamburg
Bremen
IJsselmeer
NETHERLANDS
NIEDERSACHSEN
EAST GERMANY
Oder (Odra)
Amsterdam
The Hague ('s-Gravenhage)
Rotterdam
Hannover
Berlin
Poznań
Maas
Rhein
NORDRHEIN-WESTFALEN
Lippe
Zeebrugge
Dunkerque
Antwerp
Schelde
Duisburg
Essen
Dortmund
Ruhr
Düsseldorf
Cologne (Köln)
Bonn
Brussels (Brüssel / Bruxelles)
Lille
BELGIUM
Leipzig
Dresden
Wrocław (Breslau)
Ardennes
HESSEN
WEST GERMANY
Frankfurt
Mosel
LUXEMBOURG
Luxembourg
RHEINLAND-PFALZ
SAARLAND
Prague (Praha)
Reims
CHAMPAGNE
LORRAINE
Nürnberg
CZECH
ČESKÉ ZEMĚ
BADEN
BAYERN
Stuttgart
Danube
FRANCE
Seine
Vosges
ALSACE
Schwarzwald
WÜRTTEMBURG
BOURGOGNE
Saône
Munich (München)
Vienna (Wien)
Dijon
Salzburg
Zürich
FRANCHE-COMTÉ
Jura
LIECHTENSTEIN
Vaduz
Bern
Innsbruck
Brenner 1370
AUSTRIA
Grossglockner 3798
SWITZERLAND
Rhein
Jungfrau 4158
2112 St Gotthard
ALPS
Geneva (Genève)
Rhône
Simplon 2009
Matterhorn 4477
4807 Mt Blanc
Lyon
SAVOIE
ITALY
Alpi Dolomitiche
Ljubljana
DAUPHINÉ
Grenoble
Milan (Milano)
Venice (Venezia)
Zagreb
Turin (Torino)
G. di Venezia
YUG

Gulf of Riga
Riga
LATVIYSKAYA S.S.R.
Velikiye-Luki
SEA
R.S.F.S.R.
Daugavpils
LITOVSKAYA S.S.R.
Smolensk
Dnepr
R.S.F.S.R.
Gulf of Gdańsk
Vilnius
Gdynia
Minsk
BELORUSSKAYA S.S.R.
Bobruysk
Dneprovskaya
Białystok
Gomel
OLAND
Dnepr
Vistula (Wisla)
Nizmennost'
Warsaw (Warszawa)
Brest
Łódź
U.S.S.R.
Lublin
Wisla
Kiyev
Dnepr
Oder (Odra)
Chorzow
Kraków
L'vov
UKRAINSKAYA S.S.R.
Podol'skaya Vozv
Pridneprovskaya Vozv.
SLOVAKIA
SLOVENSKO
Košice
Dnestr
MOLDAVSKAYA S.S.R.
Nyíregyháza
Carpatii Orientali
Baia Mare
Budapest
Dnestr
Odessa
UNGARY
Cluj-Napoca
Bacău
Szeged
Arad
ROMANIA
Transylvanian Alps
(Mtii Carpatii Meridionali)
Black Sea
AVIA
Novi Sad

1:5M 0 50 100 mls

Shetland
NORWAY
Orkney
C. Wrath
Outer Hebrides
The Minch
Inverness
L. Ness
Aberdeen
SCOTLAND
Ben Nevis
1344
Grampian Mts
Dundee
L. Lomond
NORTH
SEA
Glasgow
Edinburgh
Clyde
Cheviots
Newcastle-upon-Tyne
Londonderry
N. IRELAND
Stranraer
Larne
L. Neagh
Belfast
Scafell Pike
977
Middlesbrough
Pennines
Isle of Man
IRISH SEA
Leeds
Galway
Shannon
Dublin
(Baile Atha Cliath)
Holyhead
Liverpool
Manchester
Sheffield
REP. OF
IRELAND
Wicklow Mts
1085
Snowdon
Cambrian Mts
The Wash
Norwich
WALES
Birmingham
ENGLAND
NETHERLANDS
The Hague
('s-Gravenhage)
Rotterdam
St George's Chan.
Cork
Harwich
Swansea
Cardiff
Bristol
London
Thames
Zeebrugge
Antwerp
Dover
BELGIUM
Dunkerque
Calais
Brussels
(Brüssel/
Bruxelles)
Southampton
Boulogne
Lille
ARTOIS
Plymouth
English Channel
Land's End
PICARDIE
Cherbourg
Le Havre
Channel Is
(U.K.)
NORMANDIE
Paris
Roscoff
FRANCE

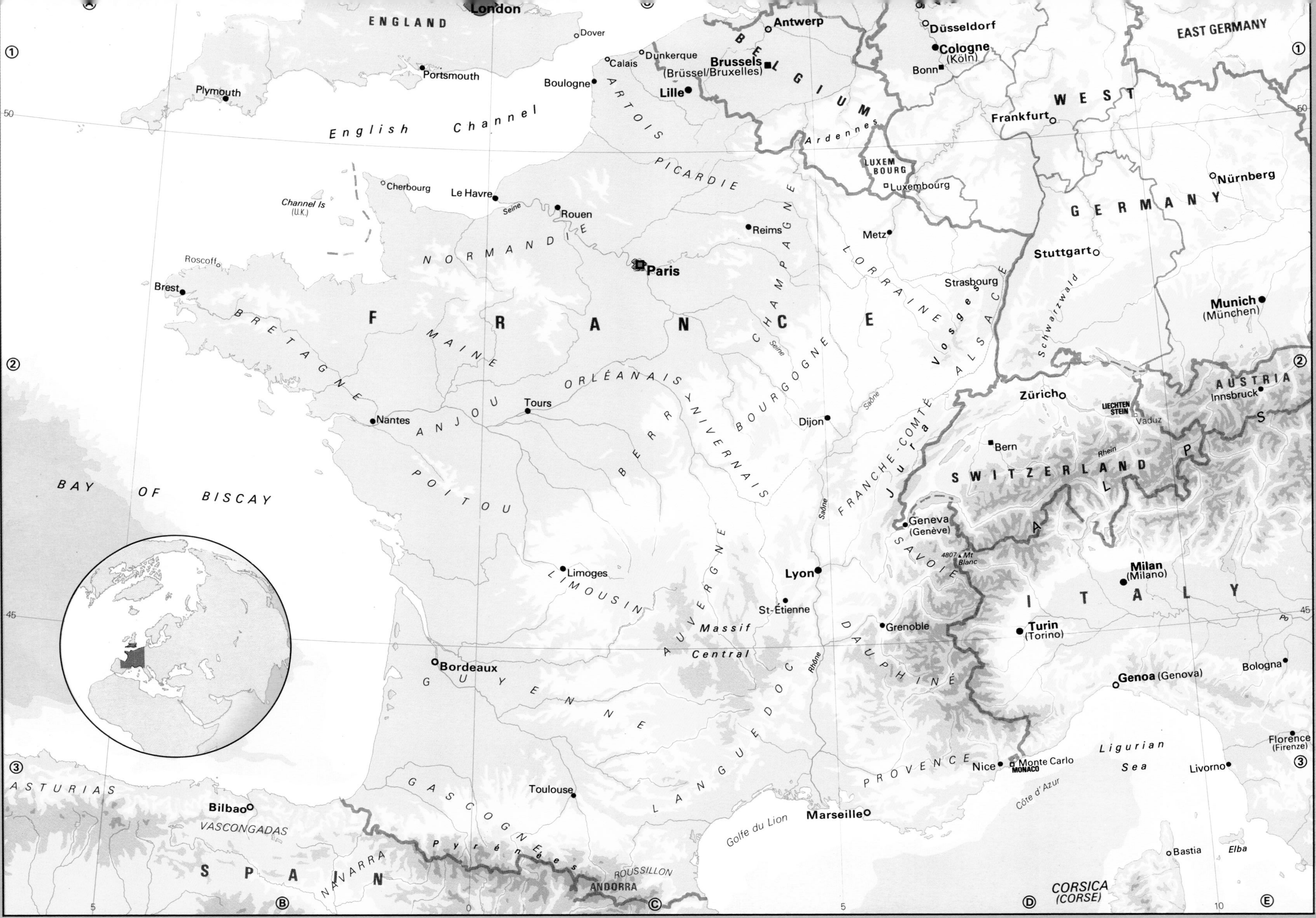

ENGLAND
London
Dover
Portsmouth
Plymouth
English Channel
Channel Is (U.K.)
Cherbourg
Le Havre
Seine
Rouen
Boulogne
Calais
Dunkerque
Lille
Brussels (Brüssel/Bruxelles)
Antwerp
BELGIUM
Ardennes
LUXEMBOURG
Luxembourg
Düsseldorf
Cologne (Köln)
Bonn
Frankfurt
WEST GERMANY
EAST GERMANY
Nürnberg
Stuttgart
Schwarzwald
Munich (München)
AUSTRIA
Innsbruck
LIECHTENSTEIN
Vaduz
Zürich
Bern
Rhein
SWITZERLAND
ALPS
Geneva (Genève)
4807 Mt Blanc
Milan (Milano)
ITALY
Turin (Torino)
Po
Bologna
Genoa (Genova)
Florence (Firenze)
Livorno
Ligurian Sea
Elba
Bastia
CORSICA (CORSE)
Monte Carlo
MONACO
Nice
Côte d'Azur
ARTOIS
PICARDIE
NORMANDIE
Paris
Reims
CHAMPAGNE
Metz
LORRAINE
Strasbourg
Vosges
ALSACE
FRANCE
BRETAGNE
Roscoff
Brest
MAINE
ANJOU
Nantes
Tours
ORLÉANAIS
BERRY
NIVERNAIS
BOURGOGNE
Seine
Dijon
Saône
FRANCHE-COMTÉ
Jura
SAVOIE
Lyon
St-Étienne
Grenoble
DAUPHINÉ
POITOU
BAY OF BISCAY
Limoges
LIMOUSIN
AUVERGNE
Massif Central
Rhône
Bordeaux
GUYENNE
LANGUEDOC
PROVENCE
Marseille
Golfe du Lion
Toulouse
GASCOGNE
Pyrénées
ROUSSILLON
ANDORRA
ASTURIAS
Bilbao
VASCONGADAS
NAVARRA
SPAIN
50
45
5
0
5
10

0 50 100 mls
Munich (München)
WEST GERMANY
Vienna (Wien)
Salzburg
Basel
Zürich
LIECHTENSTEIN
Vaduz
Bern
Innsbruck
Brenner 1370
A U S T R I A
Graz
Jura
S W I T Z E R L A N D
2112 St Gotthard
Geneva (Genève)
Simplon 2009
Matterhorn 4477
Mt Blanc
St Bernard
Lyon
Alpi Dolomitiche
Ljubljana
Zagreb
F R A N C E
Col du Mt Cenis 2803
Milan (Milano)
Verona
Venice (Venezia)
G. di Venezia
Turin (Torino)
C R O A T I A
Velebit
Genoa (Genova)
MONACO
Ligurian Sea
SAN MARINO
Florence (Firenze)
Livorno
Ancona
Marseille
Split (Spalato)
D A L M A
Y U
A D R I A T I C
Bastia
Elba
Pescara
Ajaccio
CORSICA (CORSE)
Civitavecchia
Rome (Roma)
Olbia
Sassari
Naples (Napoli)
Vesuvio 1277
S A R D I N I A (S A R D E G N A)
TYRRHENIAN SEA
Cagliari
Cosenza
Stromboli
S I C I L Y (S I C I L I A)
Palermo
Messina
Reggio di Calabria
Etna 3323
Syracuse (Siracusa)
Bone ('Annaba)
Constantine
Tunis
A L G E R I A
T U N I S I A
MALTA
M E D I T E R R A N E A N S

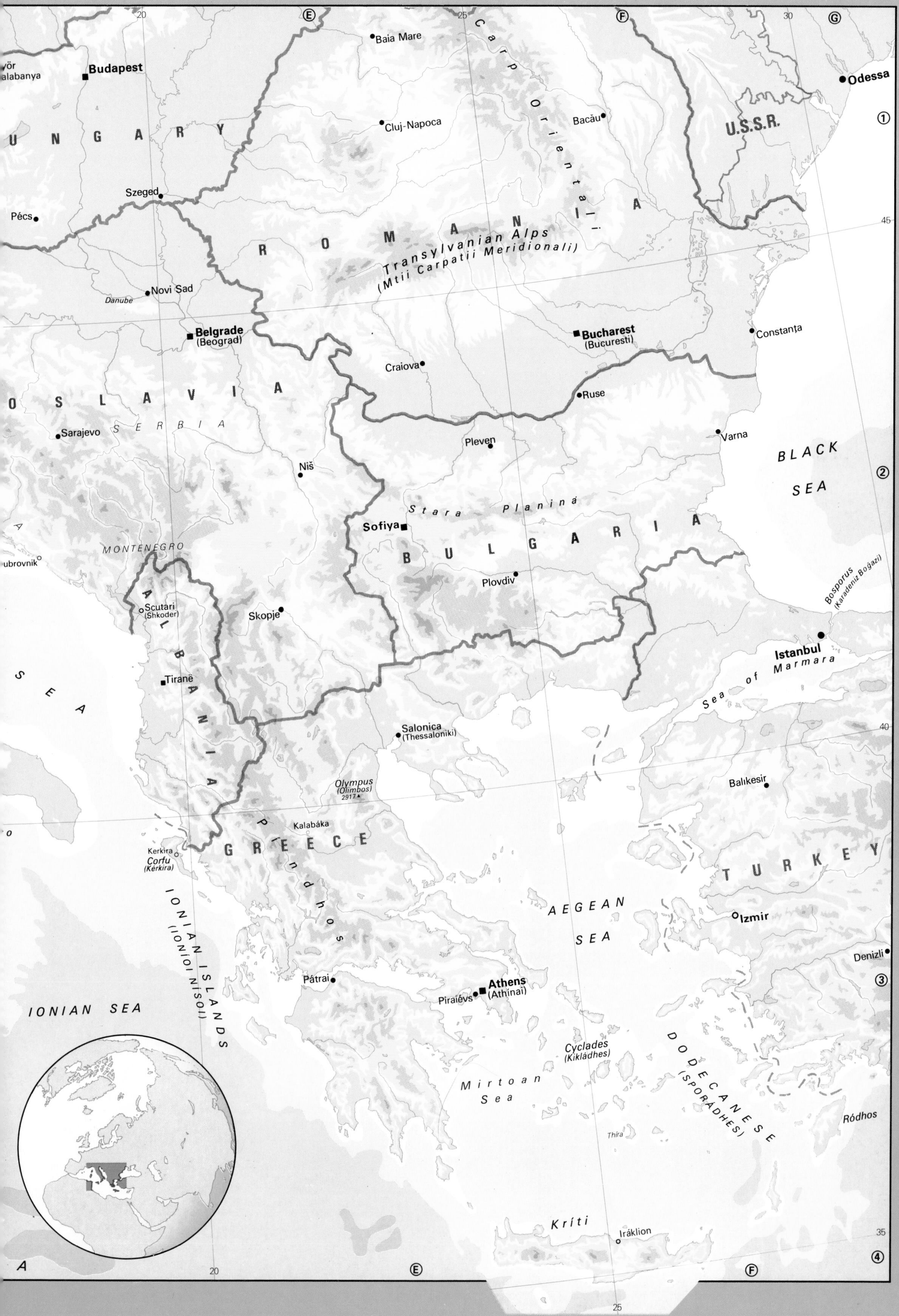

20
E
25
F
30
G
Baia Mare
Carpatii Orientali
Budapest
alabanya
Odessa
Cluj-Napoca
Bacău
U.S.S.R.
1
UNGARY
Szeged
Pécs
ROMANIA
45
Transylvanian Alps
(Mtii Carpatii Meridionali)
Novi Sad
Danube
Belgrade
(Beograd)
Bucharest
(Bucuresti)
Constanța
Craiova
OSLAVIA
Ruse
Sarajevo
SERBIA
Varna
Pleven
BLACK SEA
Niš
2
Stara Planina
Sofiya
BULGARIA
MONTENEGRO
ubrovnik
Plovdiv
Bosporus
(Karadeniz Boğazi)
Scutari
(Shkoder)
Skopje
ALBANIA
Istanbul
Sea of Marmara
Tiranë
SEA
40
Salonica
(Thessaloniki)
Olympus
(Olimbos)
2917
Balıkesir
Pindhos
Kalabáka
GREECE
Kerkira
Corfu
(Kérkira)
TURKEY
IONIAN ISLANDS
(IONIOI NISOI)
AEGEAN SEA
Izmir
Denizli
3
Pátrai
Athens
(Athínai)
Piraiévs
IONIAN SEA
Cyclades
(Kikládhes)
DODECANESE
(SPORÁDHES)
Mirtoan Sea
Ródhos
Thíra
Kríti
Iráklion
35
A
4

BAY OF BISCAY
FRANCE
SPAIN
PORTUGAL
MOROCCO
ALGERIA
MEDITERRANEAN SEA
BALEARIC ISLANDS (ISLAS BALEARES)
Menorca
Mallorca
Ibiza
Palma de Mallorca
La Coruna
Oviedo
Santander
Bilbao
León
Burgos
Valladolid
Oporto (Porto)
Zaragoza
Lérida
Barcelona
Tarragona
Perpignan
Marseille
Andorra-La-V.
ANDORRA
Madrid
Castellon de la P.
Valencia
Albacete
Alicante
Murcia
Lisbon (Lisboa)
Tagus (Tejo)
Badajoz
Córdoba
Seville (Sevilla)
Granada
Malaga
Cádiz
Faro
Gibraltar (U.K.)
Str. of Gibraltar
Tangier (Tanger)
Melilla (Sp.)
Oran
Algiers (Alger)
GALICIA
ASTURIAS
Cordillera Cantabrica
VASCONGADAS
NAVARRA
Pyrénées
Pirineos
CATALUÑA
ARAGÓN
LEÓN
CASTILLA LA VIEJA
CASTILLA LA NUEVA
EXTREMADURA
La Mancha
MURCIA
VALENCIA
Sierra Morena
ANDALUCIA
Sa Nevada
Costa Brava
Costa Blanca
Costa del Sol
Costa de la Luz

1 Bedouin tent in the Sahara

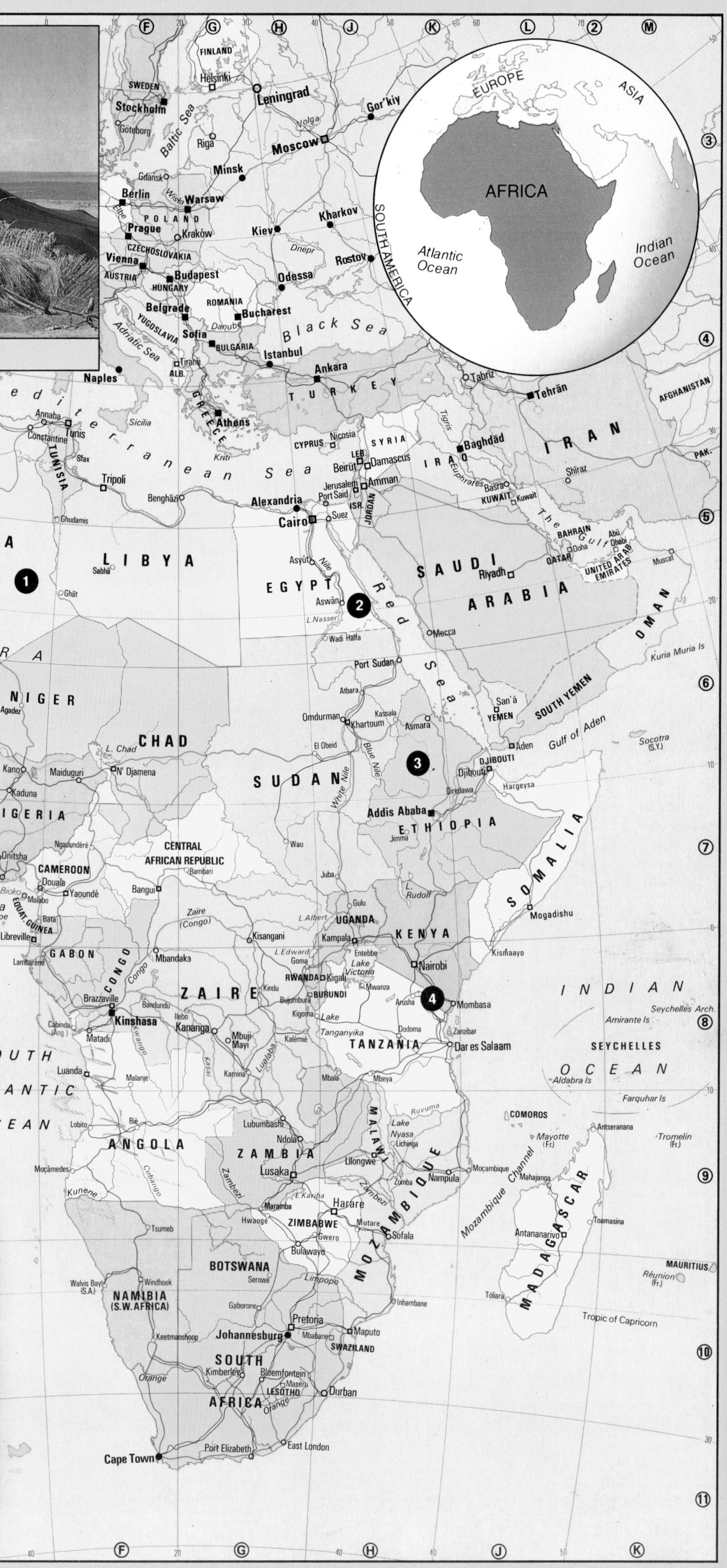

2 The River Nile, Aswan, Egypt

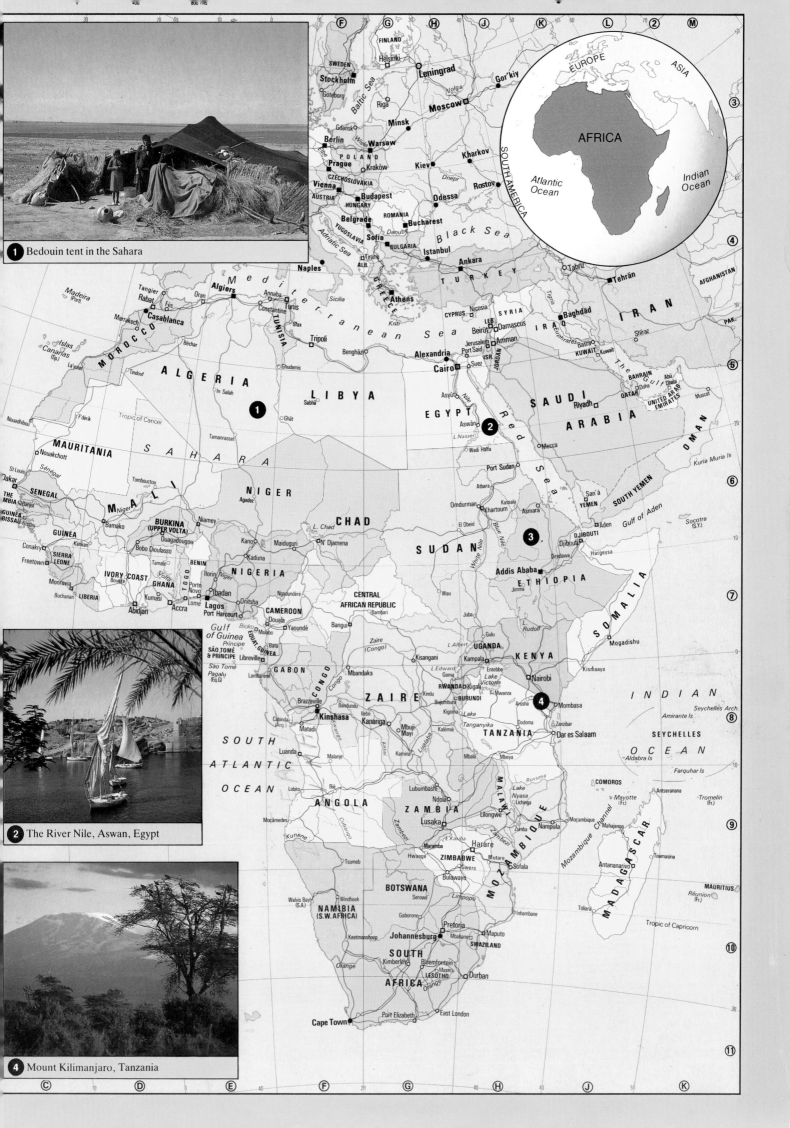

4 Mount Kilimanjaro, Tanzania

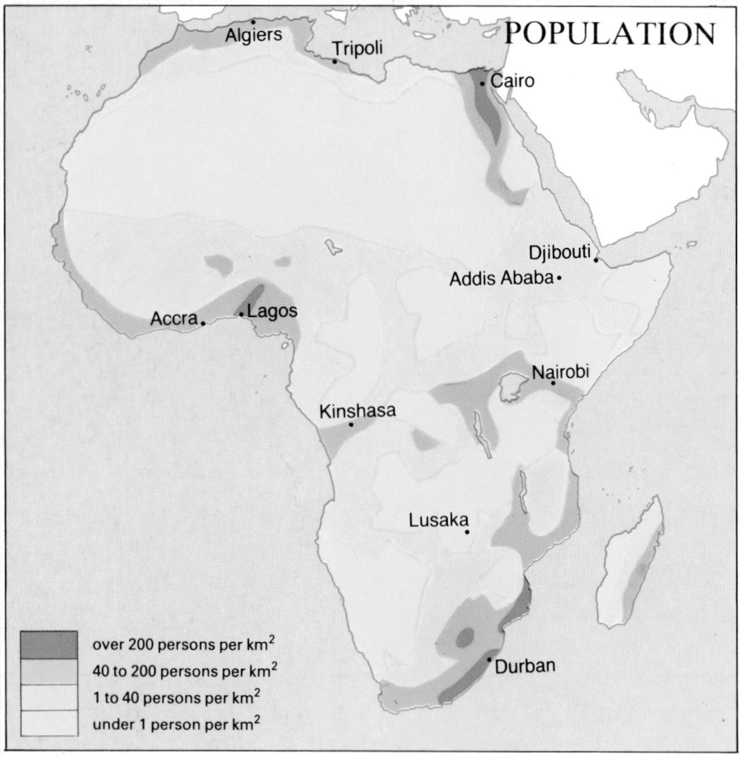

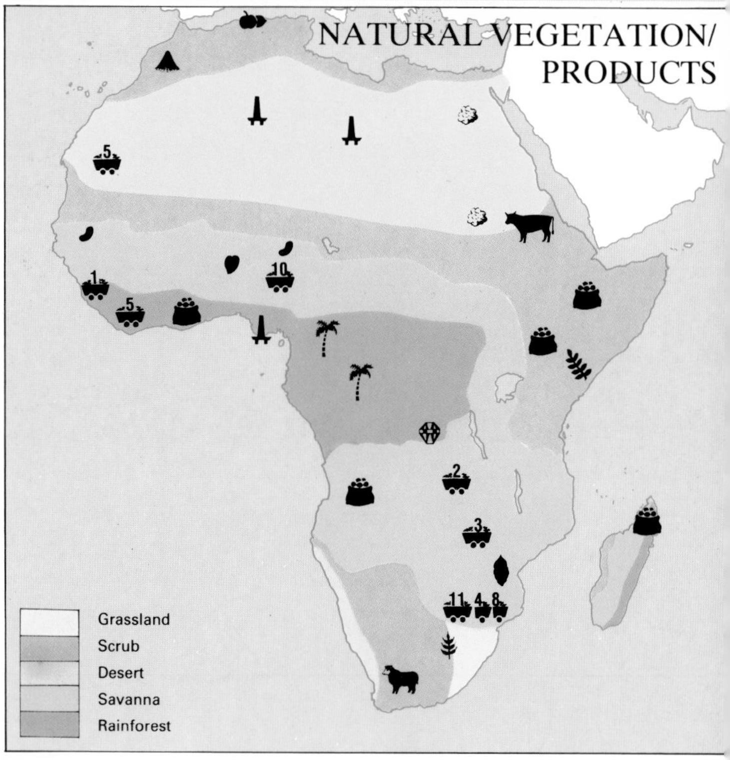

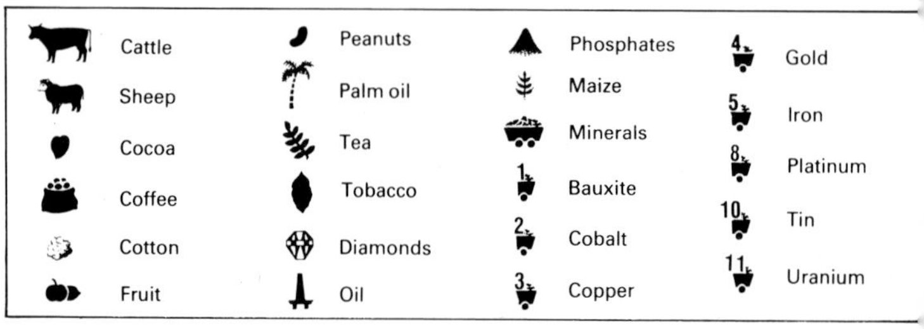

DID YOU KNOW THAT ...?

1 The largest desert in the world is the Sahara, but only about 30% of it is sand! The rest is rocky waste. People live mainly near oases, where the land is watered by springs rising to the surface and crops can be grown. The desert is very hot and dry, but there are a few plants and animals (like camels) specially adapted to these conditions.

2 The Nile is the longest river in the world and flows for 6650 km (4132 miles) through North Africa to the Mediterranean Sea. The Nile used to flood its banks each year, but now the High Dam at Aswan controls the floods. When the dam was built, the temples of Abu Simbel (3000 years old) were moved to a higher site to stop them being flooded.

3 Some parts of Africa have had no rain, or very little, for several years. Food crops have failed and many people have died from malnutrition and starvation. A further problem has been wars, which have driven many people from their homes and fields. Even if part of a country can grow food, it is difficult to move that food into areas where none can be grown. There are few lorries and, where people are at war, transporting food may be dangerous. Although western countries have sent food supplies, there is still not enough to feed the hundreds of thousands of people who are starving. Governments are trying to find ways of growing more food and distributing it more quickly.

4 Kilimanjaro (now renamed Uhuru, meaning 'freedom') is the highest mountain in Africa (5895 m; 19 340 feet) and its peaks are always covered in snow.

EGYPT

Area: 1 000 250 sq km
(386 197 sq miles)
Population: 47 000 000
Capital: Cairo
Language: Arabic
Currency: Egyptian Pound

ETHIOPIA

Area: 1 221 918 sq km
(471 783 sq miles)
Population: 32 000 000
Capital: Addis Ababa
Language: Amharic
Currency: Birr

KENYA

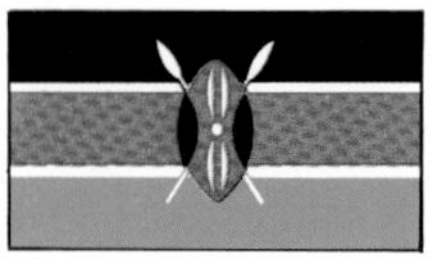

Area: 582 644 sq km
(224 959 sq miles)
Population: 19 400 000
Capital: Nairobi
Languages: English, Swahili
Currency: Kenya Shilling

LIBYA

Area: 1 759 530 sq km
(679 355 sq miles)
Population: 3 700 000
Capital: Tripoli
Language: Arabic
Currency: Libyan Dinar

NIGERIA

Area: 923 769 sq km
(356 667 sq miles)
Population: 88 100 000
Capital: Lagos
Language: English
Currency: Naira

SOUTH AFRICA

Area: 1 221 038 sq km
(471 443 sq miles)
Population: 31 700 000
Capital: Pretoria
Languages: Afrikaans, English
Currency: Rand

SUDAN

Area: 2 505 792 sq km
(967 486 sq miles)
Population: 21 000 000
Capital: Khartoum
Language: Arabic
Currency: Sudanese Pound

ZAIRE

Area: 2 344 885 sq km
(905 360 sq miles)
Population: 32 200 000
Capital: Kinshasa
Language: French
Currency: Zaire

Lisbon (Lisboa)
PORTUGAL
SPAIN
Azores (Acores)
Madeira (Portugal)
Canary Islands (Islas Canarias) (Spain)
Seville (Sevilla)
Str. of Gibraltar
Gibraltar (U.K.)
Tangiers (Tanger)
Ceuta (Sp.)
Tetouan
Melilla (SP.)
Algiers (Alger)
Mostaganem
El Asnam
Skikda (Philippeville)
Bône ('Annaba)
Tunis
Batna
Tlemcen
Rabat
Casablanca (El-Dar-El-Beida)
Meknès
Laghouat
TUNISIA
Marrakech
Haut Atlas
MOROCCO
Béchar
Ouargla
Grand Erg Occidental
El Golea
Grand erg Oriental
Tinfouchy
La'youn
ALGERIA
Erg Iguidi
Western Sahara
In Salah
Reggane
Bir Moghrein
Tropic of Cancer
SAHARA
Troudenni
Tamanrasset
El Djouf
El Khenachich
Tassili du Hoggar
MAURITANIA
Tessalit
Nouakchott
MALI
Niger
NIGER
Dakar
SENEGAL
Mopti
Tahoua
GAMBIA
Niamey
Zinder
BURKINA (UPPER VOLTA)
Bamako
Sokoto
Bissau
GUINEA BISSAU
Ouagadougou
Volta Noire
Volta Blanche
Kano
GUINEA
Bobo Dioulasso
Bolgatanga
Kaduna
Kankan
Conakry
Black Volta
White Volta
Tamale
SIERRA LEONE
Freetown
TOGO
BENIN
NIGERIA
IVORY COAST
Bouaké
GHANA
Ibadan
L. Volta
LIBERIA
Kumasi
Benin City
Enugu
Monrovia
Lagos
Porto Novo
Lomé
Abidjan
Accra
Bight of Benin
Takoradi
Port Harcourt
Mouths of the R. Niger
CAMEROON
Douala
Yaoundé
Bight of Biafra
GULF OF GUINEA
EQUATORIAL GUINEA
Bata
S.TOME & PRINCIPE
Libreville
Equator
CAPE VERDE

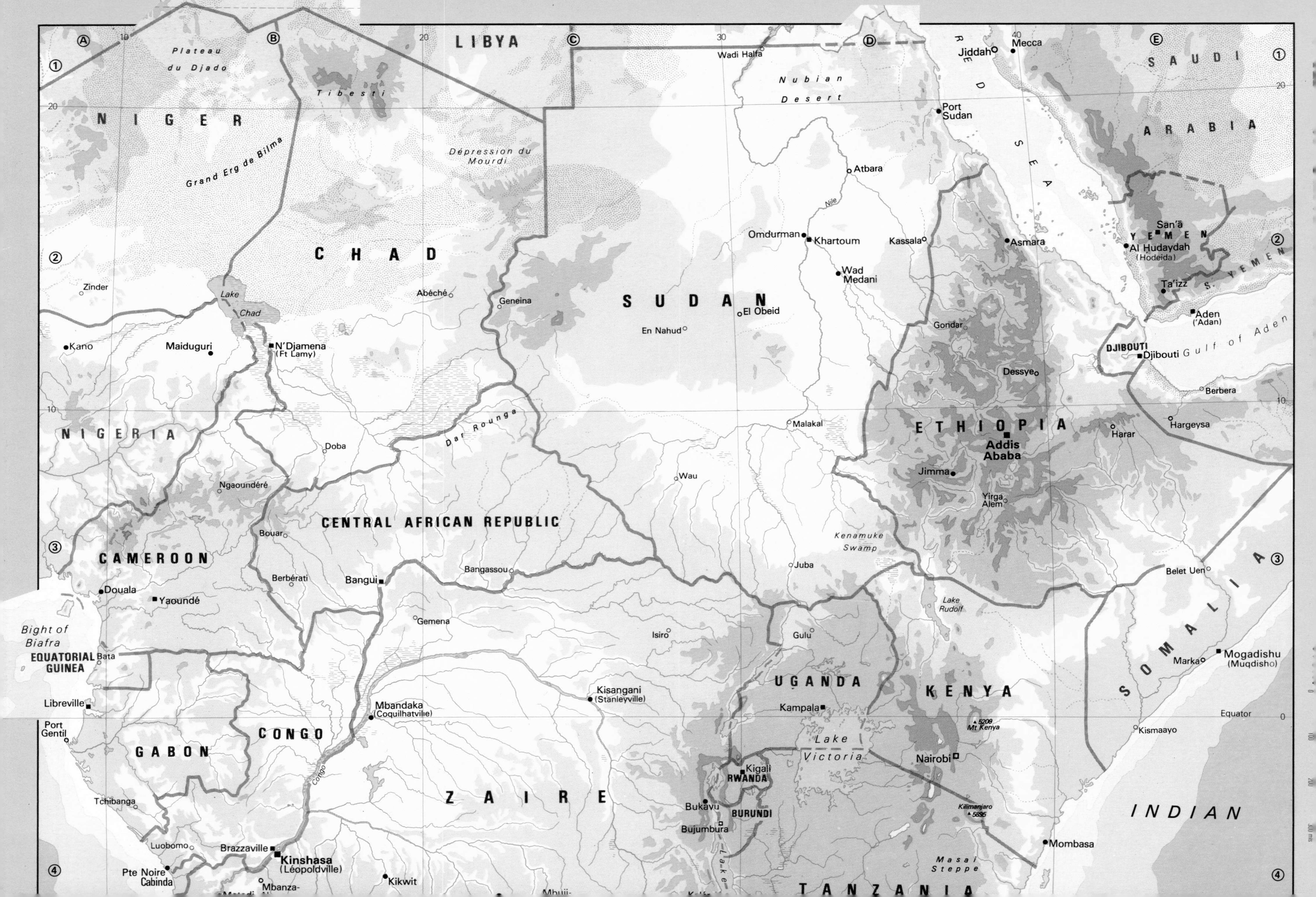
LIBYA
NIGER
CHAD
SUDAN
ETHIOPIA
SAUDI ARABIA
YEMEN
S. YEMEN
DJIBOUTI
SOMALIA
KENYA
UGANDA
RWANDA
BURUNDI
TANZANIA
ZAIRE
CONGO
GABON
EQUATORIAL GUINEA
CAMEROON
NIGERIA
CENTRAL AFRICAN REPUBLIC
INDIAN
RED SEA
Gulf of Aden
Bight of Biafra
Plateau du Djado
Tibesti
Grand Erg de Bilma
Dépression du Mourdi
Nubian Desert
Dar Rounga
Kenamuke Swamp
Lake Chad
Lake Rudolf
Lake Victoria
Lake
Masai Steppe
Nile
Congo
Wadi Halfa
Port Sudan
Jiddah
Mecca
Atbara
Omdurman
Khartoum
Kassala
Asmara
Wad Medani
El Obeid
En Nahud
Geneina
Abéché
Zinder
Kano
Maiduguri
N'Djamena (Ft Lamy)
San'ā
Al Hudaydah (Hodeida)
Ta'izz
Aden ('Adan)
Djibouti
Berbera
Hargeysa
Harar
Gondar
Dessye
Addis Ababa
Jimma
Yirga Alem
Malakal
Wau
Doba
Ngaoundéré
Bouar
Berbérati
Bangui
Bangassou
Juba
Belet Uen
Douala
Yaoundé
Bata
Libreville
Port Gentil
Gemena
Isiro
Gulu
Kisangani (Stanleyville)
Mbandaka (Coquilhatville)
Kampala
Marka
Mogadishu (Muqdisho)
Equator
Kismaayo
5209 Mt Kenya
Nairobi
Kigali
Bukavu
Bujumbura
Kilimanjaro 5895
Tchibanga
Luobomo
Brazzaville
Kinshasa (Léopoldville)
Pte Noire
Cabinda
Mbanza-
Kikwit
Mombasa
Mbuji-
A
B
C
D
E
1
2
3
4
10
20
30
40
0
100
200
300 mls

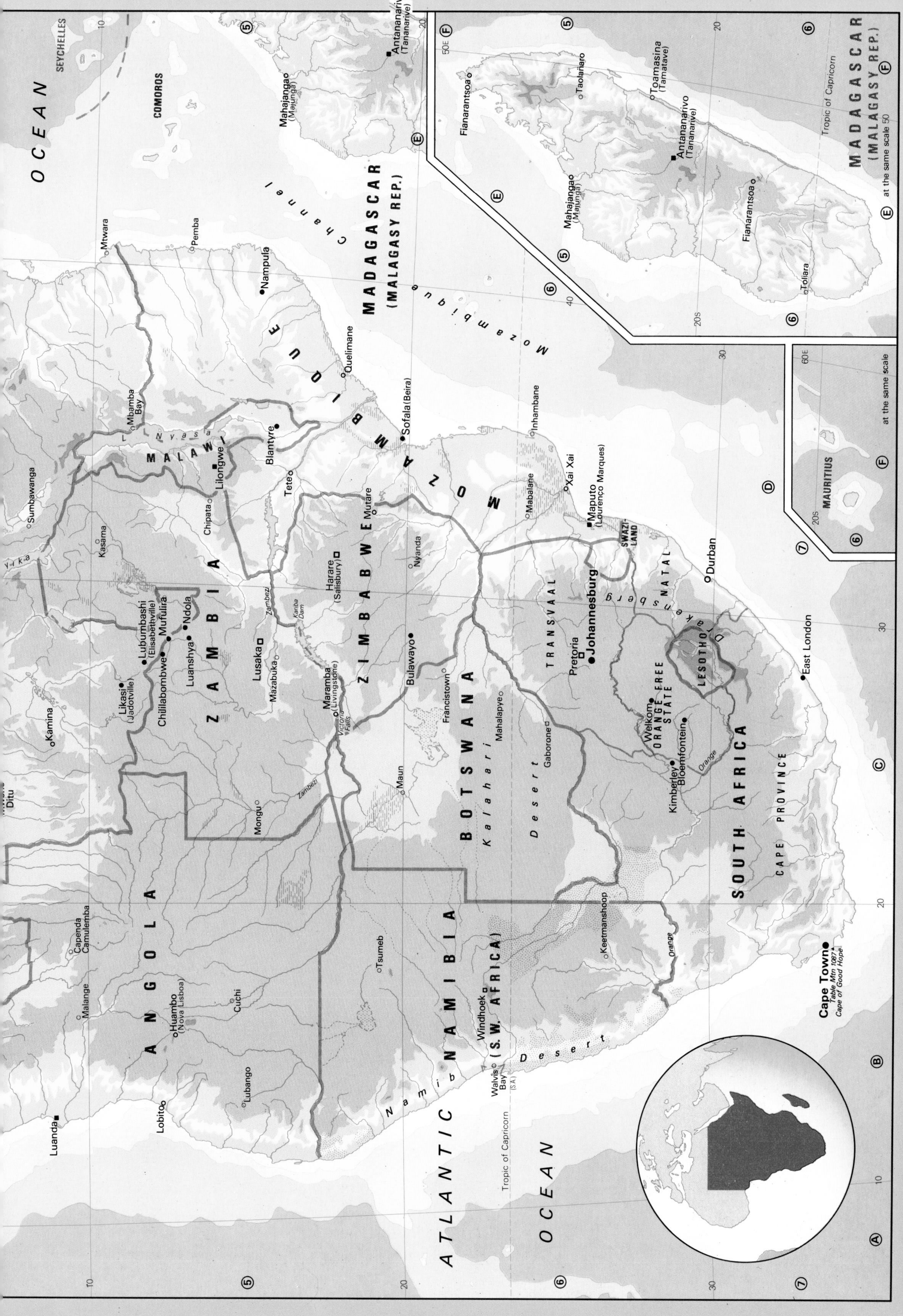
ATLANTIC OCEAN
OCEAN
ANGOLA
ZAMBIA
MALAWI
MOZAMBIQUE
ZIMBABWE
BOTSWANA
NAMIBIA (S.W. AFRICA)
SOUTH AFRICA
LESOTHO
SWAZI-LAND
MADAGASCAR (MALAGASY REP.)
SEYCHELLES
COMOROS
MAURITIUS
TRANSVAAL
ORANGE FREE STATE
NATAL
CAPE PROVINCE
Kalahari Desert
Namib Desert
Mozambique Channel
Drakensberg
L. Nyasa
Zambezi
Orange
Kariba Dam
Victoria Falls
Tropic of Capricorn
Luanda
Lobito
Lubango
Huambo (Nova Lisboa)
Cuchi
Malange
Capenda Camulemba
Ditu
Kamina
Likasi (Jadotville)
Lubumbashi (Elisabethville)
Chililabombwe
Mufulira
Luanshya
Ndola
Kasama
Sumbawanga
Mtwara
Pemba
Nampula
Quelimane
Mbamba Bay
Lilongwe
Blantyre
Chipata
Tete
Lusaka
Mazabuka
Mongu
Maramba (Livingstone)
Harare (Salisbury)
Mutare
Nyanda
Bulawayo
Francistown
Mahalapye
Maun
Gaborone
Tsumeb
Windhoek
Walvis Bay (S.A.)
Keetmanshoop
Sofala (Beira)
Inhambane
Mabalane
Xai Xai
Maputo (Lourenco Marques)
Pretoria
Johannesburg
Welkom
Bloemfontein
Kimberley
Durban
East London
Cape Town
Table Mtn 1087
Cape of Good Hope
Mahajanga (Majunga)
Antananarivo (Tananarive)
Fianarantsoa
Taolanaro
Toamasina (Tamatave)
Toliara
at the same scale

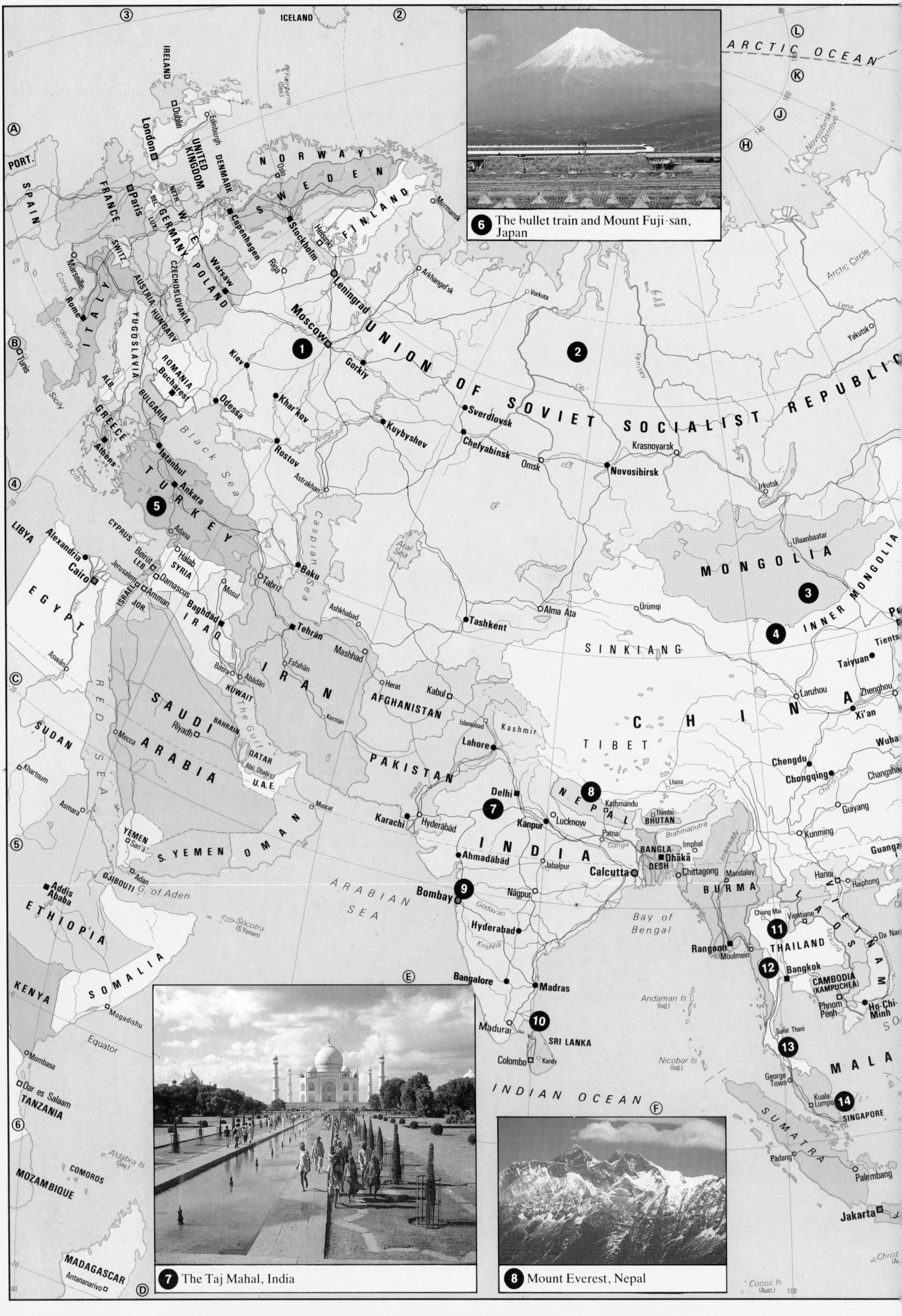

6 The bullet train and Mount Fuji-san, Japan

7 The Taj Mahal, India

8 Mount Everest, Nepal

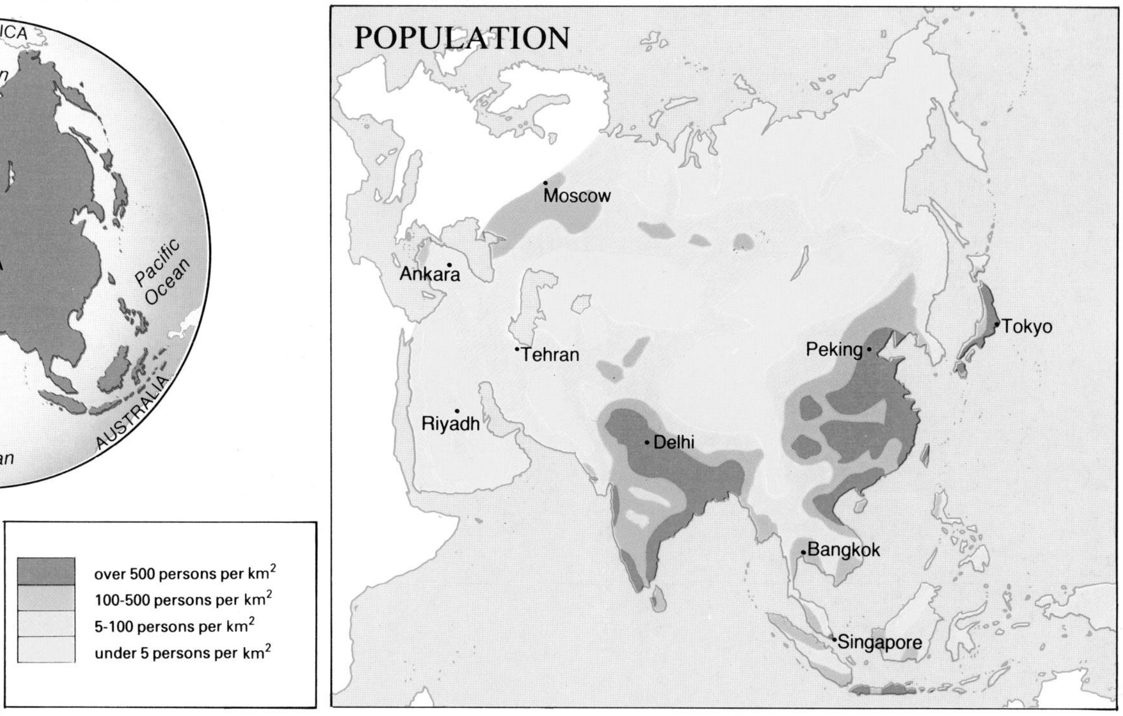

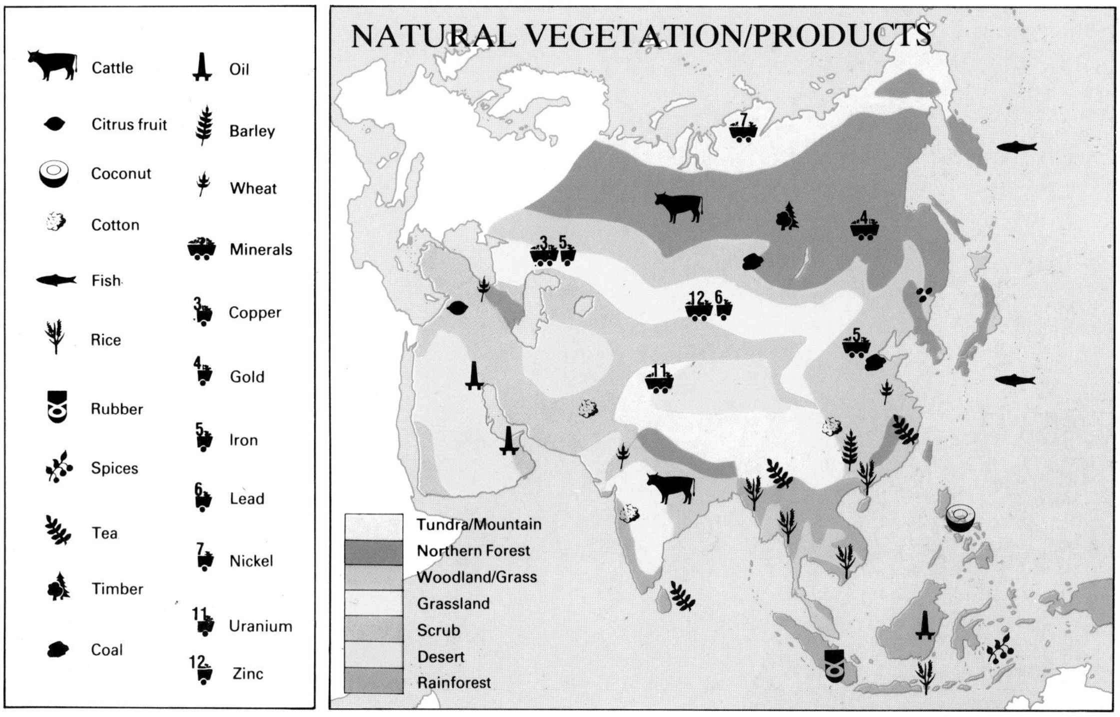

DID YOU KNOW THAT …?

1 The world's heaviest bell is the *Czar Bell* in Moscow's Kremlin. It weighs a massive 196 tonnes (193 tons) and is 5.87 m (19 ft 3 in) high! The bell was cast in 1735. It is now cracked, and hasn't been rung since 1836.

2 In Siberia, USSR, there is a huge forest called the *taiga*, which makes up a quarter of the total area of forest in the world! The trees are mostly evergreens – pine and larch. Few people used to live in the taiga, as it is a very cold area, but because it is rich in minerals more people are moving into the forest. They live in industrial towns being built deep in its heart, to exploit the minerals.

3 The huge Gobi Desert covers much of Mongolia. The Gobi is a cold, barren region of rocky plains and hills. Water is very scarce and only a few nomads live here. They exist mainly by cattle raising and live in an unusual tent called a *yurt*, which is shaped like an upside-down bowl.

4 The Great Wall of China stretches for 3460 km (2150 miles), making it the longest in the world. It was built for defence in the 3rd century BC and kept in good repair until 400 years ago. Although part of the wall was blown up to make a dam in 1979, the many remaining sections of the wall are still impressive.

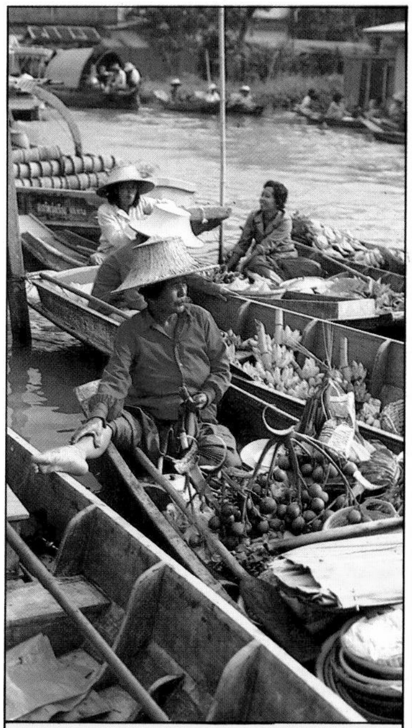

11 Floating vegetable market, Thailand

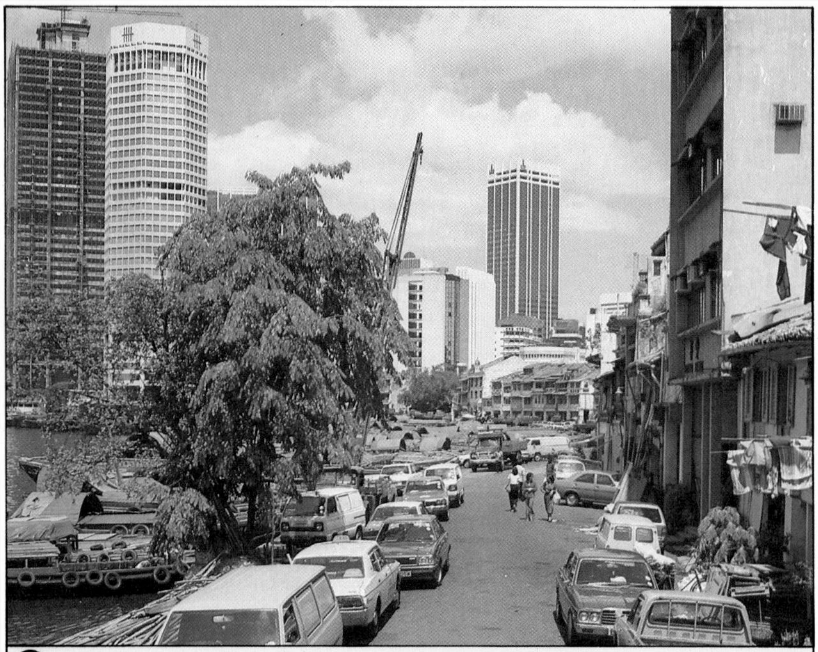

14 Singapore

12 Bangkok, Thailand

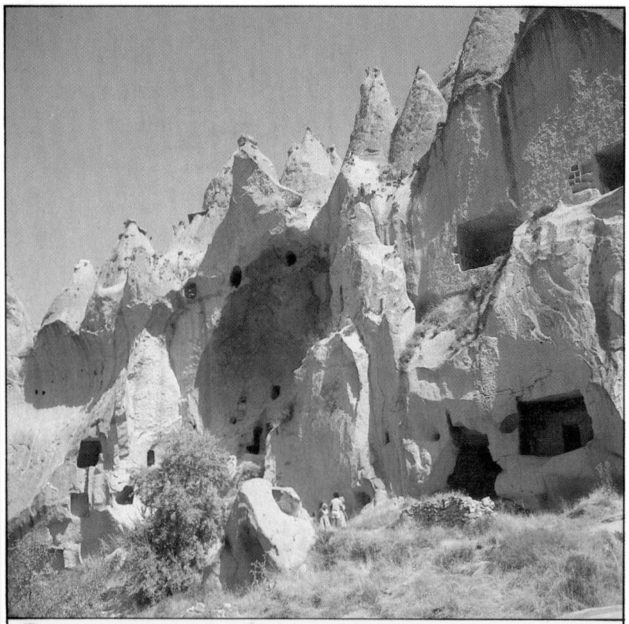

5 Cliff dwellings in Cappadocia, Turkey

13 Water buffalo ploughing Chinese paddy fields

DID YOU KNOW THAT …?

5 In central Turkey, near Urgup in the region called Cappadocia, an extraordinary landscape can be seen. There was once a plateau here, made up of layers of rock, some hard and some much softer. Over thousands of years the softer rocks have been eroded by the weather, by streams and even by men digging out caves to live in. The rocks are now shaped into strange cones, towers and 'mushrooms', with 'hats' of harder rock balancing on top! There are also complete 'villages' of caves connected to each other by passageways cut through the rock. Each cave has 'cupboards' and 'shelves' cut into its walls. Here many centuries ago people hid from religious persecution. Over 300 churches which they dug out of the rock have been found. Some people still live in caves in this region today.

6 The Seikan Tunnel in Japan is the longest tunnel in the world! It is an underwater tunnel, stretching for 54 km (34 miles). It was built for Japan's famous *bullet train*, the first passenger train to travel at 200 kph.

7 There should have been two Taj Mahals in India – a black one and a white one! In 1648, Emperor Shah Jahan completed the present Taj Mahal. It was a tomb for his wife, and made of white marble. He then began building a tomb of black marble for himself. Before work had got very far, he was overthrown.

8 At 8848 m (29 028 ft) the peak of Mt Everest in the Himalayas is the Earth's highest point! In May 1953, New Zealander Sir Edmund Hillary was the first man to climb Everest. Twenty two years later, in 1975, the first woman to reach the summit was Junko Tabei of Japan.

9 In India cows are sacred animals and are allowed to wander freely, even in the centre of big cities! Drivers are used to going round cows lying peacefully in the middle of the road.

10 Banyan trees can be seen in India and Sri Lanka. They are very unusual to look at, because what seems to be several trees growing close together, is actually just one tree! Aerial roots grow down from the banyan's branches and root in the ground. They become extra 'trunks' and support a huge canopy of leaves, which gives a lot of shade, very useful in such a hot climate.

11 Throughout Asia there are areas where many people live on boats – because there is not enough room for them to live in houses on land (or they cannot afford to) or because they just prefer to live on water. In these places, even the shops are on boats!

4 The Great Wall, China

0 Banyan tree, India

9 Street in India

Bangkok, Thailand, once had many canals, called *klongs*, in-ead of roads. (The city was called e 'Venice of the East' because e klongs reminded visitors of the nals in Venice, Italy.) They were ed for transport and also helped drain the land during the rainy ason. After cars and lorries be-n to be used for transport, many the klongs were filled in to make ads. Now Bangkok has problems ith flooding when the monsoons me.

Paddy fields, the irrigated fields in which rice is grown, t their name from *padi*, the alayan word for rice. Rice is own throughout Asia in the fer-e lowlands near the equator. illions of people live in these eas, and rice is very important to em as it yields more food per acre an any other crop.

Over half the population of the world lives in Asia – that is 782 000 000 people! Some parts Asia have many people living in small area. One of the most nsely populated countries is ngapore, which has an average of 39 people for each square lometre of ground!

AFGHANISTAN

Area: 674 500 sq km
(260 424 sq miles)
Population: 14 400 000
Capital: Kabul
Languages: Pashtu, Dari, Uzbek
Currency: Afghani

CHINA

Area: 9 561 000 sq km
(3 691 502 sq miles)
Population: 1 034 500 000
Capital: Peking
Language: Chinese (Mandarin)
Currency: Yuan

INDIA

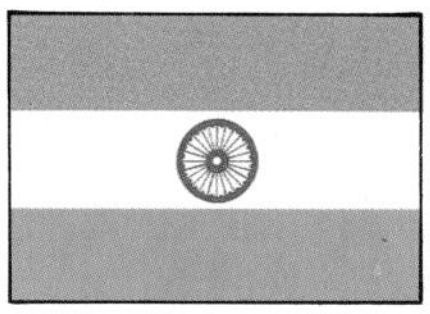

Area: 3 287 593 sq km
(1 269 340 sq miles)
Population: 746 400 000
Capital: Delhi
Languages: Hindi, English
Currency: Indian Rupee

INDONESIA

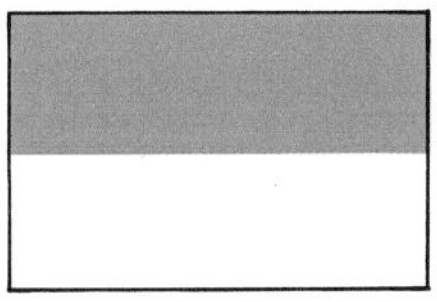

Area: 1 919 263 sq km
(741 027 miles)
Population: 161 600 000
Capital: Jakarta
Language: Bahasa (Indonesian)
Currency: Rupiah

IRAN

Area: 1 648 184 sq km
(636 364 sq miles)
Population: 43 800 000
Capital: Tehran
Language: Persian (Farsi)
Currency: Rial

IRAQ

Area: 434 924 sq km
(167 924 sq miles)
Population: 15 000 000
Capital: Baghdad
Language: Arabic
Currency: Iraqi Dinar

ISRAEL

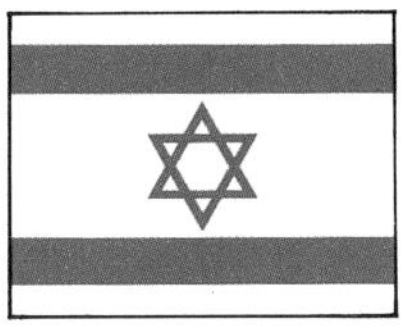

Area: 20 770 sq km
(8019 sq miles)
Population: 4 200 000
Capital: Jerusalem
Languages: Hebrew, Arabic
Currency: Shekel

JAPAN

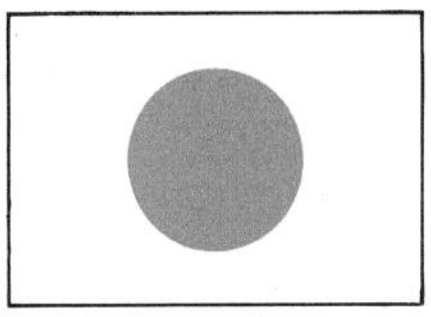

Area: 371 000 sq km
(143 243 sq miles)
Population: 119 900 000
Capital: Tokyo
Language: Japanese
Currency: Yen

MALAYSIA

Area: 330 669 sq km
(127 671 sq miles)
Population: 15 300 000
Capital: Kuala Lumpur
Language: Malay
Currency: Ringgit (Malaysian Dollar)

PAKISTAN

Area: 803 941 sq km
(310 402 sq miles)
Population: 97 300 000
Capital: Islamabad
Language: Urdu
Currency: Pakistan Rupee

SAUDI ARABIA

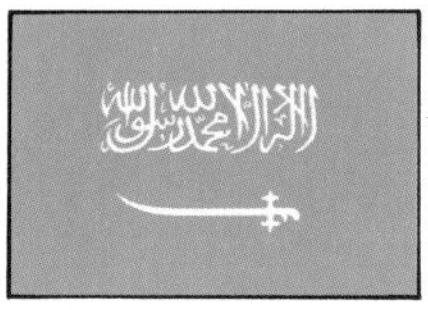

Area: 2 400 930 sq km
(927 000 sq miles)
Population: 10 800 000
Capital: Riyadh
Language: Arabic
Currency: Riyal

SINGAPORE

Area: 616 sq km
(238 sq miles)
Population: 2 500 000
Capital: Singapore
Languages: Chinese, Malay, Tamil, English
Currency: Singapore Dollar

THAILAND

Area: 513 517 sq km
(198 269 sq miles)
Population: 51 700 000
Capital: Bangkok
Languages: Thai, Chinese
Currency: Baht

TURKEY

Area: 780 576 sq km
(301 380 sq miles)
Population: 50 200 000
Capital: Ankara
Language: Turkish
Currency: Turkish Lira

USSR

Area: 22 402 000 sq km
(8 649 412 sq miles)
Population: 274 000 000
Capital: Moscow
Language: Russian
Currency: Ruble

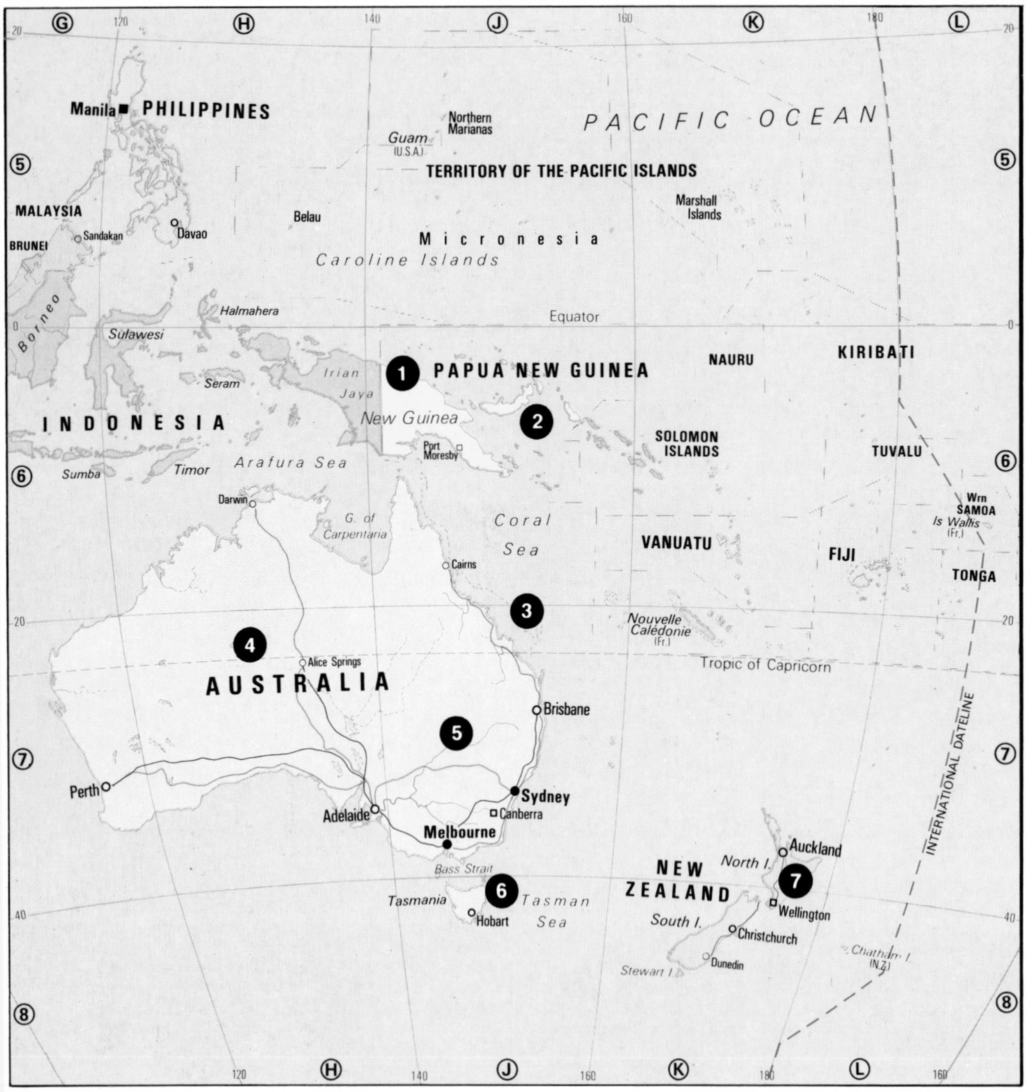

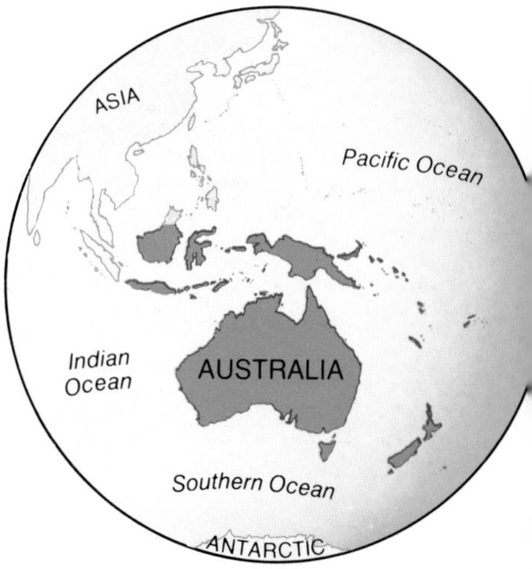

7 Geysers at Whakarewarewa, New Zealand

DID YOU KNOW THAT ...?

1 Over 700 languages are spoken in Papua New Guinea! That is more than a quarter of all the languages spoken in the world! Papua New Guinea's mountains, thick forests and islands meant that different tribes did not mix, so they did not share a common language, but instead each developed its own. Today, Pidgin English and Police Motu have become the languages which the different tribes use to talk to each other.

2 No less than 38 different species of the beautiful Bird of Paradise are to be seen in Papua New Guinea! Another 5 species are found on neighbouring islands and in northern Australia. Their tail feathers are a traditional part of Papua New Guinea tribal costume, although the birds are now protected from hunting to a great extent.

3 Australia's Great Barrier Reef is formed from the shells of millions of tiny sea creatures! It is 2000 km (1250 miles) long and is the world's biggest coral reef. There are many thousands of coral islands or *atolls* in the Pacific region.

4 Ayers Rock is a huge sandstone rock formation which rears up abruptly from the desert in central Australia. The rock is special because it changes colour with the light. Australia's native *aborigine* people believe there is something magical about the rock.

5 Australia is the driest of all the continents in the world! Rainfall is also very unevenly distributed: even though the tropical north has about 2000 mm (79 inches) a year, the centra deserts have less than 150 mi (6 inches). Irrigation is importar for agriculture, and rivers an artesian wells are used as a sourc of water. The Snowy Mountair reservoir and irrigation scheme ha brought water from the mountair to irrigate farmland in the east c Australia.

6 A Tasmanian Devil is a littl bear-like creature found onl in Tasmania. It is just 60 cm (2 f long, with a big bushy tail. It ha very sharp teeth and eats othe

4 Ayers Rock, Australia

6 Tasmanian Devil

POPULATION

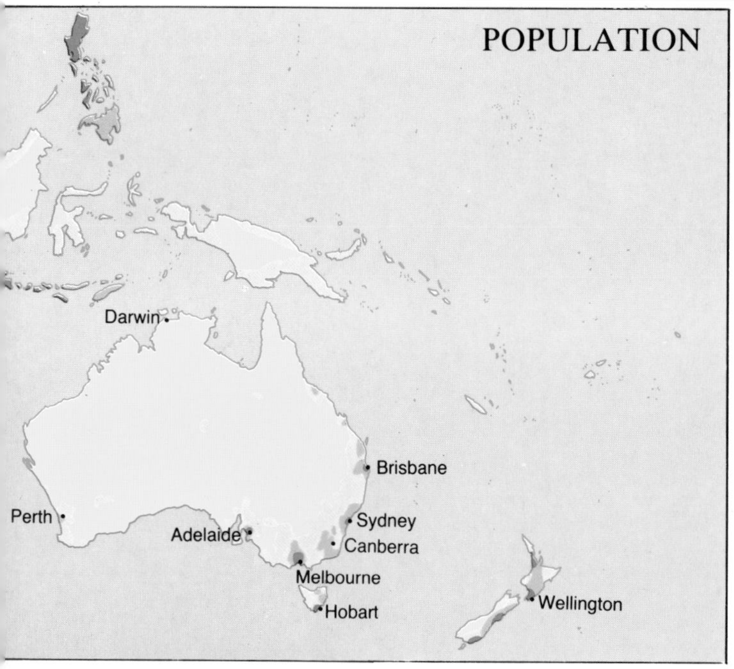

over 500 persons per km^2
100-500 persons per km^2
5-100 persons per km^2
under 5 persons per km^2

NATURAL VEGETATION/PRODUCTS

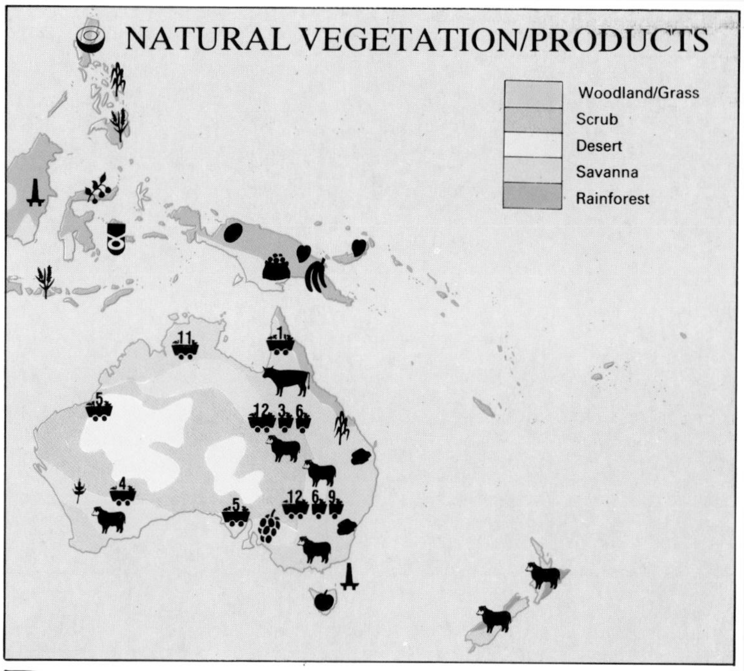

Sheep	Coffee	Coal	Minerals	6. Lead
Apples	Cocoa	Oil	1. Bauxite	9. Silver
Bananas	Rubber	Spices	3. Copper	11. Uranium
Grapes	Yams	Sugar cane	4. Gold	12. Zinc
Coconut	Rice	Wheat	5. Iron	

2 Traditional dress, Papua New Guinea

nimals and small birds when it omes out at night. The Tasmanian evil is a *marsupial*. This means it rries its young in a pouch.

7 The tallest geyser ever to have erupted was the Waimangu eyser in New Zealand. In 1904 it se to a height of 457 m (1500 ft). last erupted in 1917, killing four eople! Today, steam from New ealand's hot springs and geysers is rnessed to generate electricity.

3 The Great Barrier Reef, Australia

AUSTRALIA

Area: 7 682 300 sq km
(2 966 136 sq miles)
Population: 15 500 000
Capital: Canberra
Language: English
Currency: Australian Dollar

FIJI

Area: 18 272 sq km
(7055 sq miles)
Population: 700 000
Capital: Suva
Languages: English, Fijian
Currency: Fiji Dollar

KIRIBATI

Area: 800 sq km
(309 sq miles)
Population: 59 000
Capital: Tarawa
Languages: English, I Kiribati
Currency: Australian Dollar

NEW ZEALAND

Area: 268 675 sq km
(103 735 sq miles)
Population: 3 200 000
Capital: Wellington
Language: English
Currency: New Zealand Dollar

PAPUA NEW GUINEA

Area: 461 692 sq km
(178 259 sq miles)
Population: 3 400 000
Capital: Port Moresby
Languages: English, Melanesian Pidgin
Currency: Kina

SOLOMON ISLANDS

Area: 29 785 sq km
(11 500 sq miles)
Population: 300 000
Capital: Honiara
Languages: English, Pidgin
Currency: Solomon Islands Dollar

TONGA

Area: 699 sq km
(270 sq miles)
Population: 97 000
Capital: Nuku'alofa
Languages: English, Tongan
Currency: Pa'anga

VANUATU

Area: 14 763 sq km
(5700 sq miles)
Population: 100 000
Capital: Vila
Languages: Bislama, English, French
Currency: Australian Dollar, Vatu

WESTERN SAMOA

Area: 2831 sq km
(1093 sq miles)
Population: 200 000
Capital: Apia
Languages: Samoan, English
Currency: Tala

1:20M 0 200 400 600 800 km 0 200 400 mls

R.S.F.S.R.
1 Chuvashkaya A.S.S.R.
2 Checheno-Ingushskaya A.S.S.R.
3 Severo-Osetinskaya A.S.S.R.
4 Kabardino-Balkarskaya A.S.S.R.
GRUZINSKAYA S.S.R.
5 Abkhazskaya A.S.S.R.
6 Adzharskaya A.S.S.R.
AZERBAYDZHANSKAYA S.S.R.
7 Nakhichevanskaya A.S.S.R.
NORWEGIAN SEA
BARENTS SEA
ARCTI
KARA SEA
NORTH SEA
BALTIC SEA
BLACK SEA
CASPIAN SEA
Arctic Circle
SPITSBERGEN (Nor.)
FRANZ-JOSEF-LAND
NOVAYA ZEMLYA
Nordkapp
Glasgow
SCOTLAND
U.K.
DENMARK
Copenhagen (København)
Hamburg
GERMANY
W
E
Berlin
POLAND
Poznań
Wrocław
Łódź
Warsaw (Warszawa)
Kraków
NORWAY
Oslo
SWEDEN
Stockholm
FINLAND
Helsinki
Lappland
Murmansk
Kol'skiy Poluostrov
White Sea (Beloye More)
Arkhangel'sk
Petrozavodsk
Karel'skaya A.S.S.R.
ESTONSKAYA S.S.R.
LATVIYSKAYA S.S.R.
LITOVSKAYA S.S.R.
Riga
Novgorod
Leningrad
BELORUSSKAYA S.S.R.
Minsk
Carpathian Mts
L'vov
Dnepr
Smolensk
Moscow (Moskva)
Yaroslavl'
Vologda
Bryansk
Tula
Kolomna
UKRAINSKAYA S.S.R.
Kiyev
MOLDAVSKAYA S.S.R.
Krivoy Rog
Odessa
Dnepropetrovsk
Khar'kov
Donetsk
Zaporozh'ye
Sevastopol'
Voronezh
Saratov
Gor'kiy
Mariyskaya A.S.S.R.
Mordovskaya A.S.S.R.
Kazan
Tatarskaya A.S.S.R.
Kirov
Komi A.S.S.R.
Syktyvkar
Vorkuta
Udmurtskaya A.S.S.R.
Izhevsk
Perm'
Ufa
Bashkirskaya A.S.S.R.
Kuybyshev
Ural'sk
Volgograd
Rostov-na-Donu
Krasnodar
Novorossiysk
Maykop
Kalmytskaya A.S.S.R.
Volga
Astrakhan'
GRUZINSKAYA S.S.R.
Dagestanskaya A.S.S.R.
Tbilisi
Yerevan
ARMYANSKAYA S.S.R.
AZERBAYDZHANSKAYA S.S.R.
Baku
Tabriz
TURKEY
IRAQ
IRAN
Tehrān
Uralskiy Khrebet
ROSSIYS
Gydanskiy Poluostrov
Zapadno Sibirskaya Nizmennost
Ob'
Irtysh
Sverdlovsk
Chelyabinsk
Magnitogorsk
Omsk
Tomsk
Novosibirsk
Novokuznet
Barna
Kokchetav
Aktyubinsk
KAZAKHSKAYA S.S.R.
Semipalatinsk
Karaganda
Aral'skoye More
Kara-Kalpakskaya A.S.S.R.
Kzyl Orda
Ozero Balkhash
TURKMENSKAYA S.S.R.
UZBEKSKAYA S.S.R.
Tashkent
Alma Ata
KIRGIZSKAYA S.S.R.
Tien Shan
Pik Pobedy 7439
Leninabad
Karshi
TADZHIKSKAYA S.S.R.
Pik Kommunizma 7495
Pamir
AFGHANISTAN
SINKI

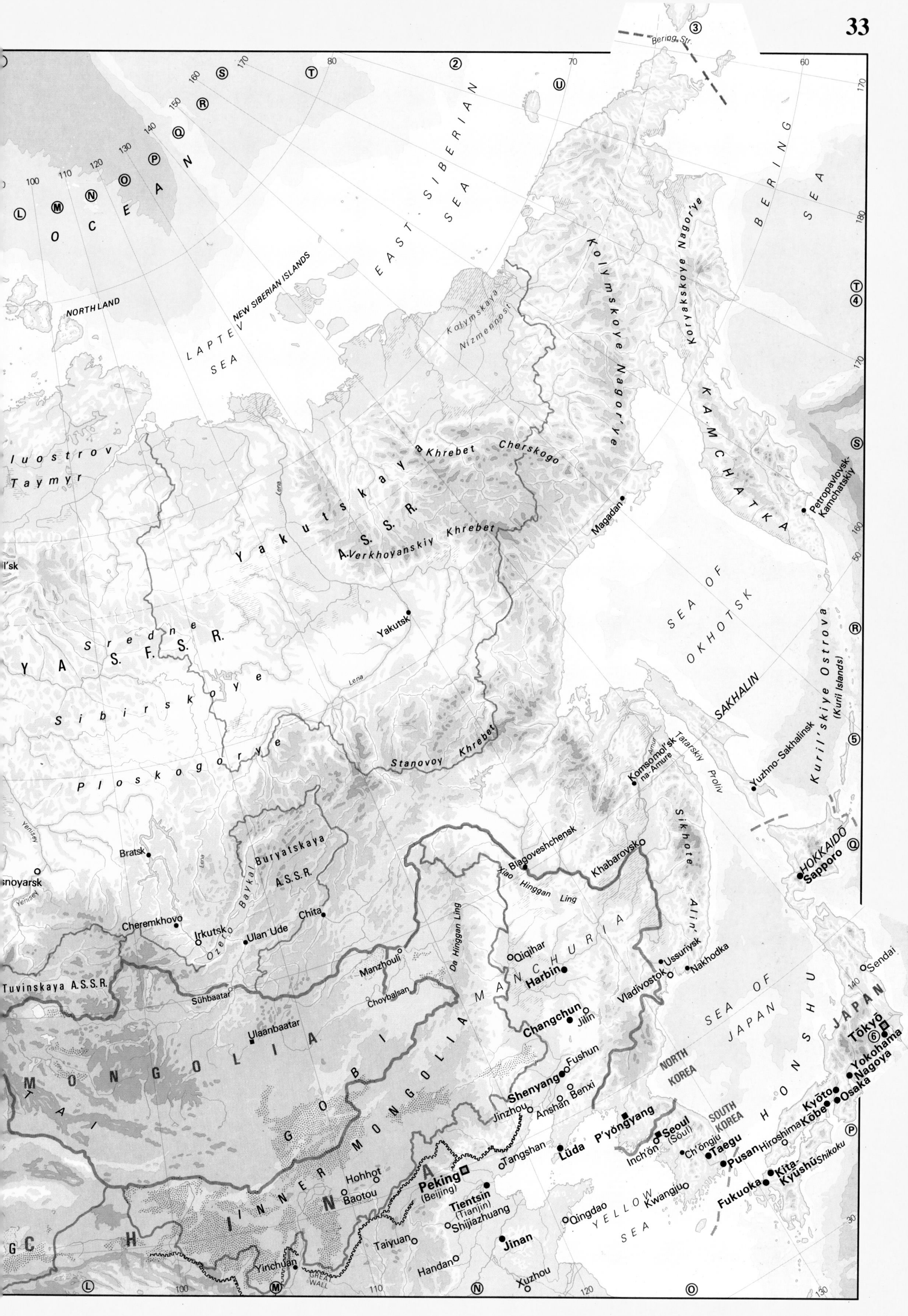
Bering Str.
OCEAN
NORTH LAND
NEW SIBERIAN ISLANDS
LAPTEV SEA
EAST SIBERIAN SEA
BERING SEA
Kolymskaya Nizmennost'
Kolymskoye Nagor'ye
Koryakskoye Nagor'ye
KAMCHATKA
Petropavlovsk-Kamchatskiy
Khrebet Cherskogo
Yakutskaya A.S.S.R.
Verkhoyanskiy Khrebet
Poluostrov Taymyr
Magadan
SEA OF OKHOTSK
Yakutsk
Lena
R.S.F.S.R.
Sredne Sibirskoye Ploskogor'ye
SAKHALIN
Kuril'skiye Ostrova (Kuril Islands)
Stanovoy Khrebet
Komsomol'sk na-Amure
Amur
Tatarskiy Proliv
Yuzhno-Sakhalinsk
Yenisey
Bratsk
Buryatskaya A.S.S.R.
Baykal Ozero
Sikhote Alin'
Blagoveshchensk
Khabarovsk
HOKKAIDO
Sapporo
Krasnoyarsk
Xiao Hinggan Ling
Cheremkhovo
Irkutsk
Ulan Ude
Chita
MANCHURIA
Da Hinggan Ling
Qiqihar
Ussuriysk
Nakhodka
Sendai
Tuvinskaya A.S.S.R.
Sühbaatar
Manzhouli
Harbin
Choybalsan
Vladivostok
SEA OF JAPAN
HONSHU
JAPAN
Changchun
Jilin
Tōkyō
Yokohama
Ulaanbaatar
MONGOLIA
Fushun
NORTH KOREA
Nagoya
Shenyang
Benxi
Kyōto
Osaka
Kobe
GOBI
Jinzhou
Anshan
P'yŏngyang
SOUTH KOREA
INNER MONGOLIA
Seoul (Soul)
Hiroshima
Tangshan
Lüda
Inch'ŏn
Ch'ŏngju
Taegu
Pusan
Kita-Kyūshū
Shikoku
Hohhot
Peking (Beijing)
Fukuoka
Baotou
Tientsin (Tianjin)
Kwangju
Qingdao
YELLOW SEA
Shijiazhuang
Taiyuan
Jinan
Handan
Yinchuan
GREAT WALL
Xuzhou

1:20M 0 200 400 600 800 km
0 200 400 mls

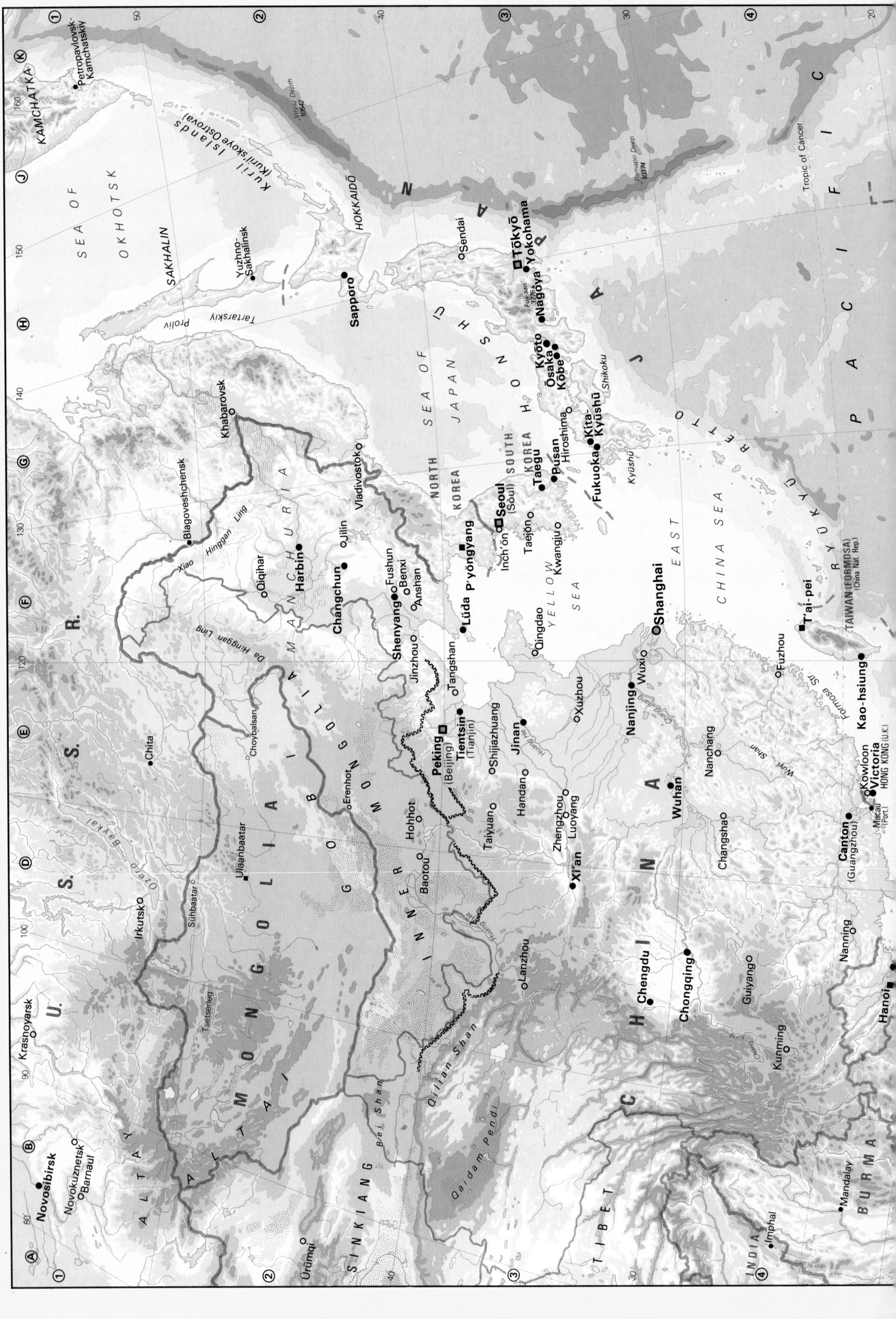
U. S. S. R.
MONGOLIA
INNER MONGOLIA
MANCHURIA
CHINA
JAPAN
NORTH KOREA
SOUTH KOREA
SINKIANG
TIBET
BURMA
INDIA
PACIFIC
SEA OF OKHOTSK
SEA OF JAPAN
YELLOW SEA
EAST CHINA SEA
KAMCHATKA
SAKHALIN
HOKKAIDŌ
HONSHŪ
Shikoku
Kyūshū
Kuril Islands (Kuril'skoye Ostrova)
RYŪKYŪ RETTO
TAIWAN (FORMOSA) (China Nat. Rep.)
HONG KONG (U.K.)
Tartarskiy Proliv
Formosa Str.
Tropic of Cancer
Vityaz Depth 10542
Ramapo Deep 10374
Fuji-san 3776
ALTAY
ALTAI
GOBI
Da Hinggan Ling
Xiao Hinggan Ling
Qilian Shan
Bei Shan
Qaidam Pendi
Ozero Baykal
Huang He
Chang Jiang
Wuyi Shan
Novosibirsk
Novokuznetsk
Barnaul
Krasnoyarsk
Irkutsk
Chita
Blagoveshchensk
Khabarovsk
Vladivostok
Petropavlovsk-Kamchatskiy
Yuzhno-Sakhalinsk
Sapporo
Sendai
Tōkyō
Yokohama
Nagoya
Kyōto
Ōsaka
Kōbe
Hiroshima
Kita-Kyūshū
Fukuoka
Seoul (Sŏul)
Inch'ŏn
Taejŏn
Taegu
Pusan
Kwangju
P'yŏngyang
Ulaanbaatar
Sühbaatar
Tsetserleg
Choybalsan
Ürümqi
Erenhot
Hohhot
Baotou
Qiqihar
Harbin
Jilin
Changchun
Fushun
Benxi
Anshan
Shenyang
Jinzhou
Lüda
Tangshan
Tientsin (Tianjin)
Peking (Beijing)
Shijiazhuang
Taiyuan
Handan
Jinan
Qingdao
Xuzhou
Zhengzhou
Luoyang
Xi'an
Lanzhou
Nanjing
Wuxi
Shanghai
Wuhan
Nanchang
Changsha
Chengdu
Chongqing
Guiyang
Kunming
Nanning
Canton (Guangzhou)
Kowloon
Victoria
Macau (Port.)
Fuzhou
T'ai-pei
Kao-hsiung
Hanoi
Mandalay
Imphal

Rangoon
Mouths of the Irrawaddy
Vientiane
THAILAND
VIETNAM
Hainan Dao
LUZON
Quezon City
Manila
PHILIPPINES
INDO-
SOUTH
CHINA
CHINA
SEA
Bangkok
CAMBODIA (KAMPUCHEA)
Mekong
Phnom Penh
Saigon (Ho Chi Minh)
Mouths of the Mekong
ANDAMAN SEA
O C E A N
Trust Terr. of the PACIFIC ISLANDS (USA)
CAROLINE ISLANDS
MINDANAO
SULU SEA
General Santos
MALAYSIA
BRUNEI
SARAWAK
Medan
Kuala Lumpur
SINGAPORE
SUMATRA
CELEBES SEA
Manado
Equator
BORNEO
KALIMANTAN
Pontianak
MOLUCCAS
CERAM SEA
CELEBES (SULAWESI)
Palembang
Banjarmasin
IRIAN JAYA
PAPUA NEW GUINEA
NEW GUINEA
JAVA SEA
Makassar (Ujung Pandang)
BANDA SEA
Jakarta
Bandung
Semarang
INDONESIA
Surabaya
Port Moresby
JAVA
ARAFURA SEA
TIMOR
Great Barrier Reef
CORAL SEA
INDIAN OCEAN
TIMOR SEA
Darwin
Cape York
Gulf of Carpentaria
AUSTRALIA
100
110
120
130
140
10
0
10

1:10M

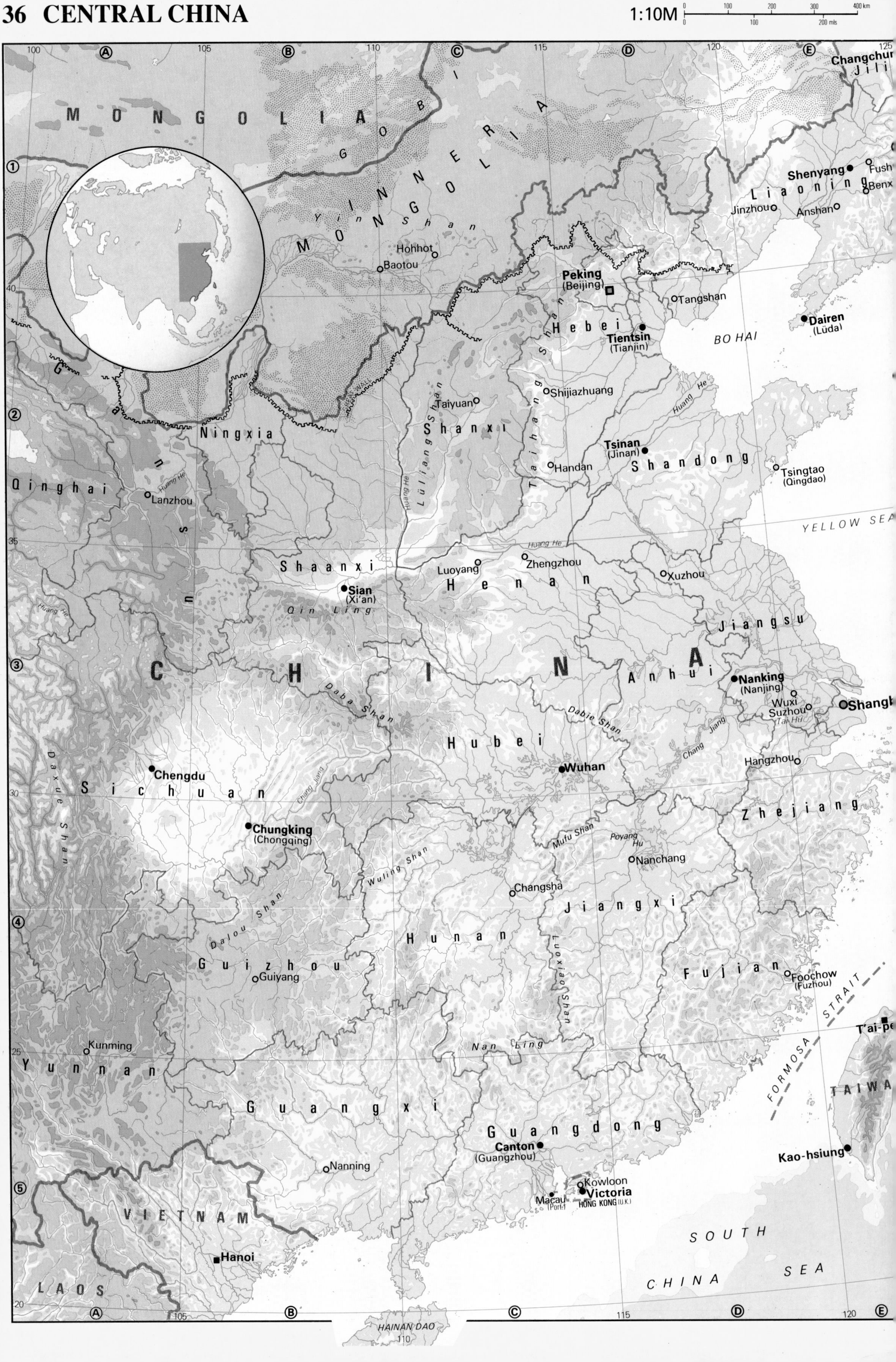
MONGOLIA
GOBI
INNER MONGOLIA
Yin Shan
Hohhot
Baotou
Changchun
Jilin
Shenyang
Fushun
Benxi
Liaoning
Jinzhou
Anshan
Peking
(Beijing)
Tangshan
Dairen
(Lüda)
Hebei
Tientsin
(Tianjin)
BO HAI
Shijiazhuang
Taiyuan
Shanxi
Lüliang Shan
Taihang Shan
Huang He
Ningxia
Gansu
Qinghai
Lanzhou
Tsinan
(Jinan)
Shandong
Handan
Tsingtao
(Qingdao)
YELLOW SEA
Shaanxi
Luoyang
Zhengzhou
Xuzhou
Sian
(Xi'an)
Henan
Qin Ling
Jiangsu
CHINA
Anhui
Nanking
(Nanjing)
Wuxi
Suzhou
Tai Hu
Shanghai
Daba Shan
Dabie Shan
Hubei
Chang Jiang
Wuhan
Hangzhou
Chengdu
Sichuan
Zhejiang
Daxue Shan
Chungking
(Chongqing)
Mufu Shan
Poyang Hu
Nanchang
Wuling Shan
Changsha
Dalou Shan
Jiangxi
Hunan
Luoxiao Shan
Guizhou
Guiyang
Fujian
Foochow
(Fuzhou)
FORMOSA STRAIT
T'ai-pei
Kunming
Nan Ling
Yunnan
TAIWAN
Guangxi
Guangdong
Canton
(Guangzhou)
Kao-hsiung
Nanning
Kowloon
Victoria
Macau
(Port.)
HONG KONG (U.K.)
VIETNAM
SOUTH CHINA SEA
Hanoi
LAOS
HAINAN DAO

1:10M 0 100 200 300 400 km 0 100 200 mls

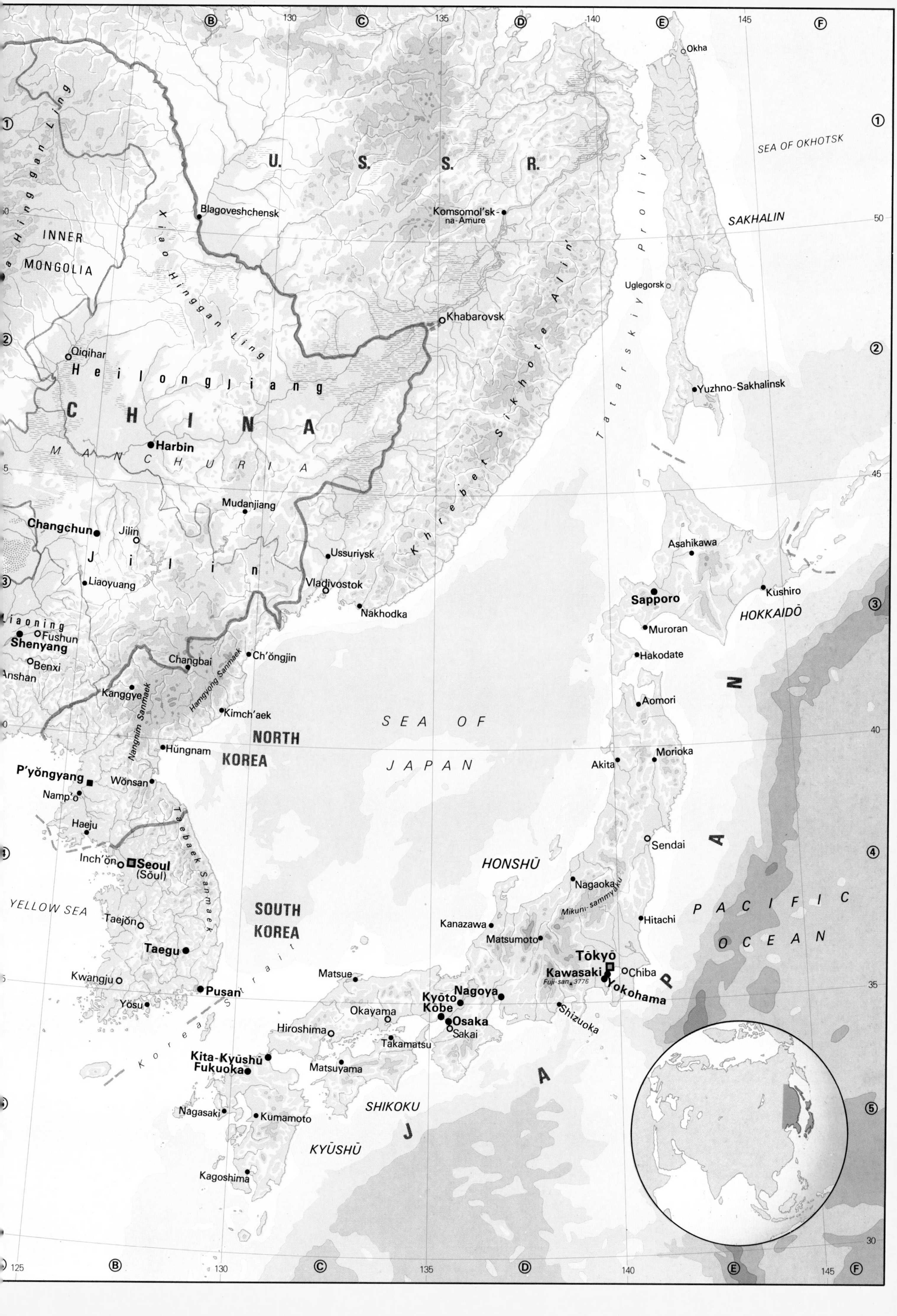

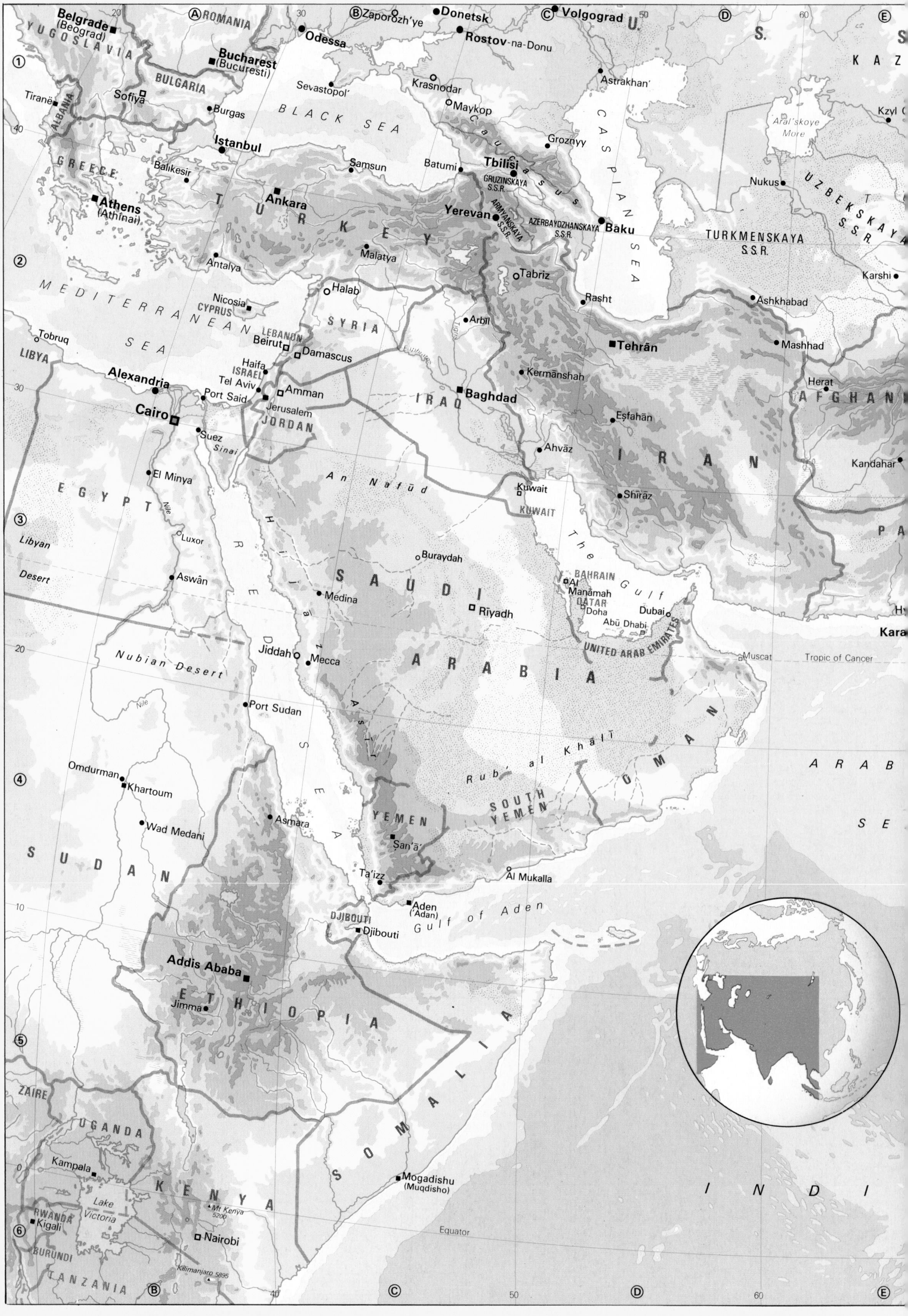

Belgrade (Beograd)
YUGOSLAVIA
ROMANIA
Bucharest (Bucuresti)
BULGARIA
Sofiya
Tiranë
ALBANIA
Burgas
BLACK SEA
Istanbul
GREECE
Balıkesir
Athens (Athínai)
Odessa
Zaporozh'ye
Donetsk
Volgograd
U.
S.
Rostov-na-Donu
Sevastopol'
Krasnodar
Maykop
Caucasus
Astrakhan'
CASPIAN SEA
Groznyy
Samsun
Batumi
Tbilisi
GRUZINSKAYA S.S.R.
ARMYANSKAYA S.S.R.
AZERBAYDZHANSKAYA S.S.R.
Yerevan
Baku
TURKEY
Ankara
Malatya
Antalya
KAZ
Kzyl
Aral'skoye More
Nukus
UZBEKSKAYA S.S.R.
TURKMENSKAYA S.S.R.
Karshi
Ashkhabad
Mashhad
Herat
AFGHAN
Kandahar
MEDITERRANEAN SEA
Nicosia
CYPRUS
Halab
SYRIA
LEBANON
Beirut
Damascus
Haifa
ISRAEL
Tel Aviv
Amman
Jerusalem
JORDAN
Tobruq
LIBYA
Alexandria
Port Said
Cairo
Suez
Sinai
Tabriz
Rasht
Tehrān
Arbil
Tigris
Kermānshah
Baghdad
IRAQ
Eşfahān
Ahvāz
IRAN
Shīrāz
Kuwait
KUWAIT
An Nafūd
El Minya
EGYPT
Nile
Luxor
Libyan Desert
Aswân
Buraydah
Hijaz
SAUDI ARABIA
Medina
Rīyadh
BAHRAIN
Al Manāmah
QATAR
Doha
The Gulf
Dubai
Abū Dhabi
UNITED ARAB EMIRATES
Muscat
Tropic of Cancer
PA
Hy
Kara
Nubian Desert
Jiddah
Mecca
Port Sudan
Asir
RED SEA
Rub' al Khali
OMAN
ARAB
SE
Omdurman
Khartoum
Wad Medani
SUDAN
Asmara
YEMEN
Şan'ā'
SOUTH YEMEN
Ta'izz
Al Mukalla
Aden ('Adan)
Gulf of Aden
DJIBOUTI
Djibouti
Addis Ababa
ETHIOPIA
Jimma
SOMALIA
ZAIRE
UGANDA
Kampala
KENYA
Lake Victoria
Mt Kenya 5200
RWANDA
Kigali
BURUNDI
Nairobi
Mogadishu (Muqdisho)
Equator
INDI
Kilimanjaro 5895
TANZANIA

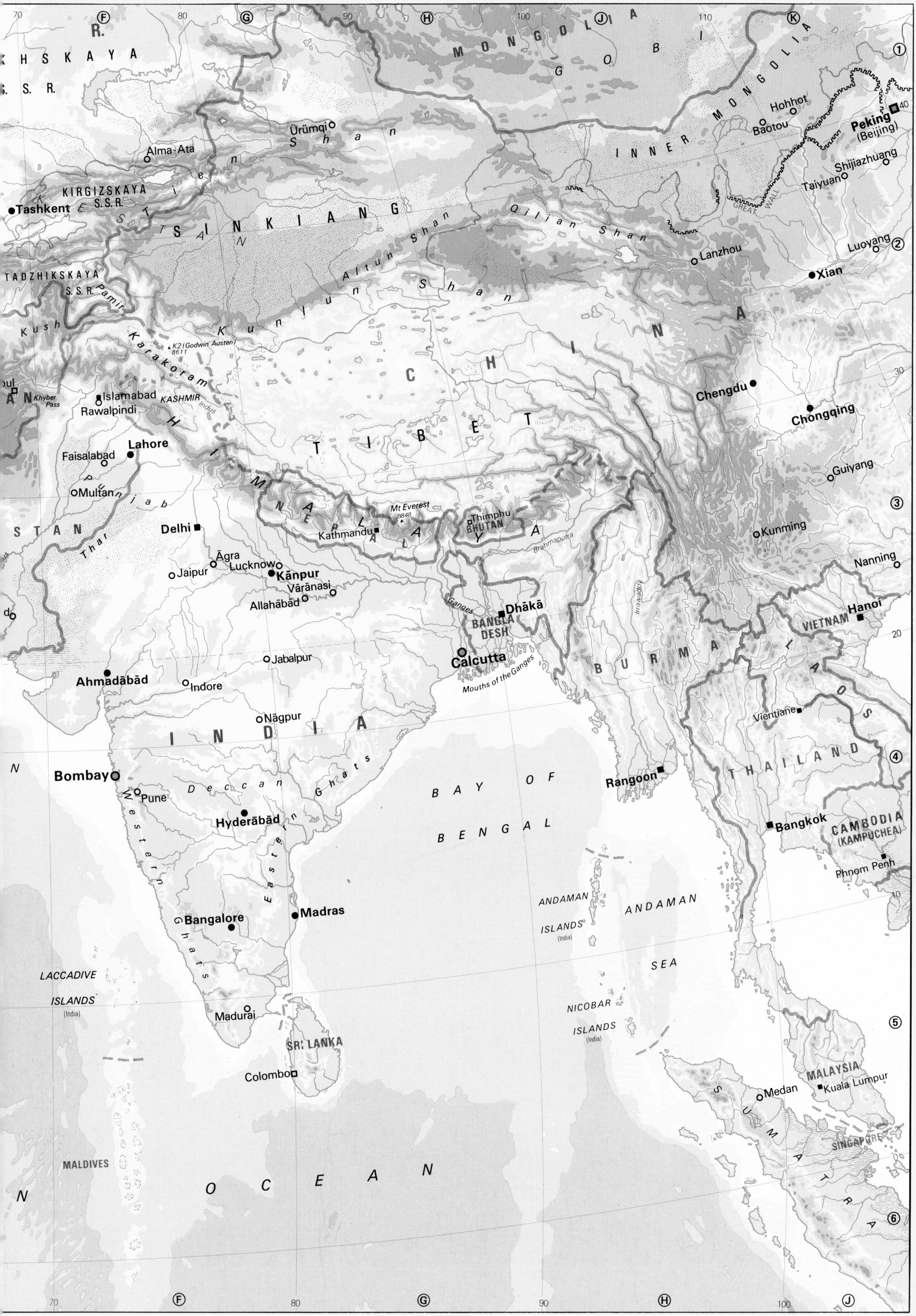
MONGOLIA
GOBI
INNER MONGOLIA
Hohhot
Baotou
Peking
(Beijing)
Shijiazhuang
Taiyuan
GREAT WALL
Luoyang
Xian
Lanzhou
Qilian Shan
Ürümqi
Tien Shan
Alma-Ata
KIRGIZSKAYA S.S.R.
Tashkent
SINKIANG
TADZHIKSKAYA S.S.R.
Pamir
Altun Shan
Kunlun Shan
Karakoram
K2 (Godwin Austen) 8611
Khyber Pass
Islamabad
Rawalpindi
KASHMIR
Indus
Lahore
Faisalabad
Multan
Punjab
Thar
Delhi
Jaipur
Āgra
Lucknow
Kānpur
Vārānasi
Allahābād
HIMALAYA
NEPAL
Kathmandu
Mt Everest 8848
Thimphu
BHUTAN
Brahmaputra
TIBET
CHINA
Chengdu
Chongqing
Guiyang
Kunming
Nanning
Hanoi
VIETNAM
LAOS
Vientiane
THAILAND
Bangkok
CAMBODIA
(KAMPUCHEA)
Phnom Penh
BURMA
Irrawaddy
Rangoon
Ganges
Dhākā
BANGLA DESH
Calcutta
Mouths of the Ganges
Jabalpur
Indore
Ahmadābād
Nāgpur
INDIA
Bombay
Pune
Deccan
Western Ghats
Eastern Ghats
Hyderābād
Madras
Bangalore
Madurai
SRI LANKA
Colombo
LACCADIVE ISLANDS
(India)
MALDIVES
BAY OF BENGAL
ANDAMAN ISLANDS
(India)
ANDAMAN SEA
NICOBAR ISLANDS
(India)
SUMATRA
Medan
MALAYSIA
Kuala Lumpur
SINGAPORE
OCEAN

0 100 200 mls
BURMA
Mandalay
Myingyan
Meiktila
Taung-gyi
Irrawaddy
Pyinmana
Prome
Henzada
Pegu
Bassein
Rangoon
Moulmein
Mouths of the Irrawaddy
Tavoy
ANDAMAN SEA
Mergui Archipelago
NICOBAR ISLANDS (India)
Banda Aceh
CHINA
Nanning
Pingxiang
Lao Cai
Maomin
Zhanjiang
Hanoi
Haiphong
Gulf of Tongkin
Haikou
HAINAN
Ya Xian
LAOS
Mekong
Luang Prabang
Vinh
Vientiane
Udon Thani
VIETNAM
INDO CHINA
Hue
Da Nang
THAILAND
Chiang Mai
Muang Phrae
M.Phitsanulok
Ubon Ratchathani
Pakse
Nakhon Ratchasima
Khong
Bangkok
Thon Buri
Sisophon
Qui Nhon
CAMBODIA (KAMPUCHEA)
Ban Me Thuot
B.Hua Hin
Nha Trang
Da Lat
Cam Ranh
Kompong Cham
Phnom Penh
GULF OF THAILAND
Chau Phu
Saigon (Ho Chi Minh)
My Tho
Vung Tau
Rach Gia
Can Tho
Mouths of the Mekong
Surat Thani
SOUTH CHINA SEA
Ban Hat Yai
Kota Bharu
George Town
Strait of Malacca
Kuala Trengganu
MALAYSIA
Ipoh
MALAYA
Medan
PENINSULAR MALAYSIA
Kelang
Kuala Lumpur
Pematangsiantar
SUMATRA
Simeulue
Melaka
SARAWAK (Malaysia)
Johor Bharu
SINGAPORE
Kuching
Padangsidempuan
Nias
Singkawang
Pekanbaru
BORNEO
Equator
Pontianak
Rengat
P.P.Batu
INDONESIA
Padang
Siberut
Jambi
95
100
105
110
20
15
10
5
0

1:7.5M 0 100 200 300 km; 0 50 100 150 mls

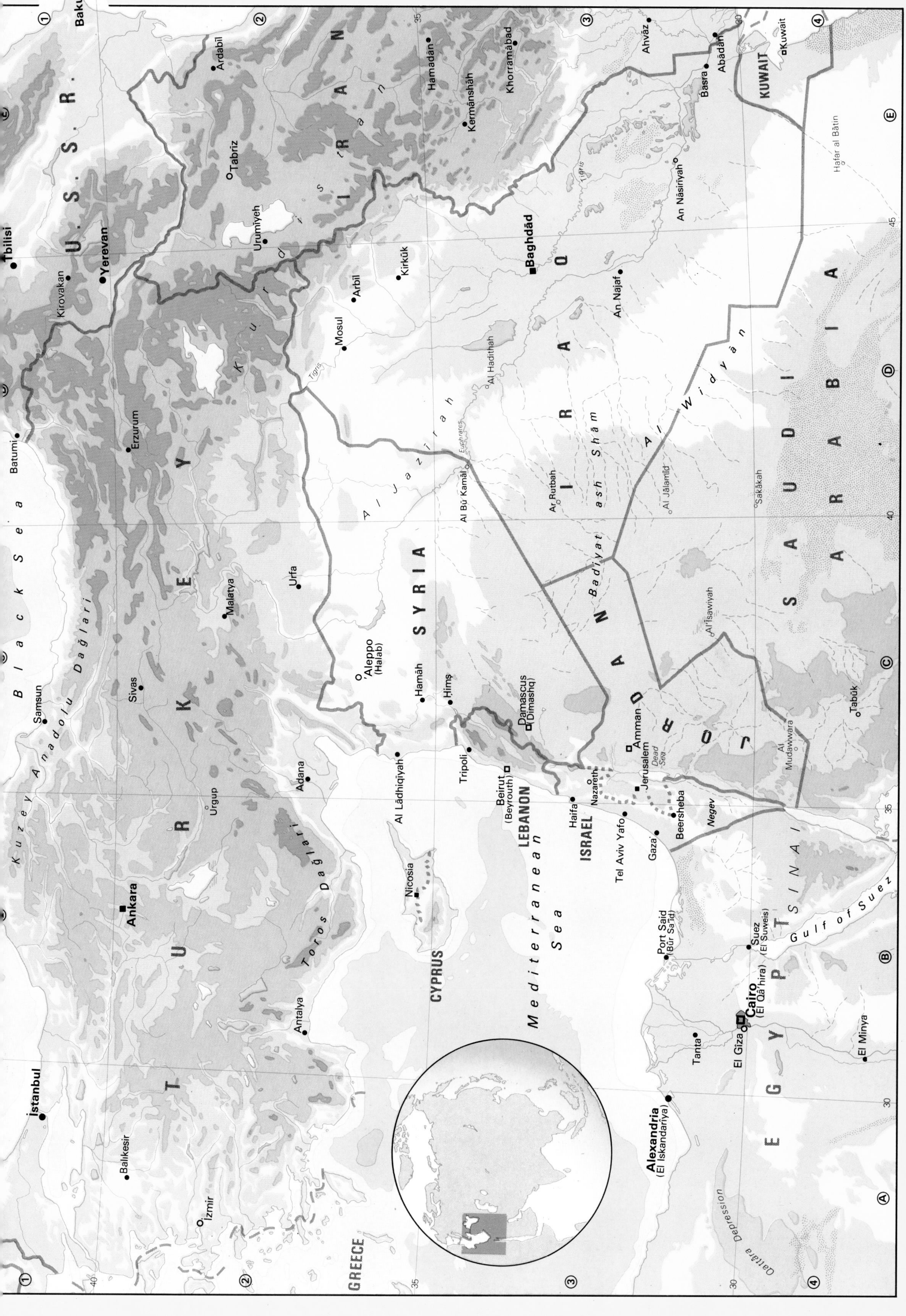

0
200
400 mls
BORNEO
Balikpapan
Manado
Halmahera
MOLUCCAS
CELEBES (SULAWESI)
I N D O N E S I A
Banda Sea
IRIAN JAYA
Pegunungan Maoke
NEW GUINEA
Bismarck Archipelago
PAPUA NEW GUINEA
Port Moresby
Timor
Arafura Sea
Torres Strait
Timor Sea
Darwin
Gulf of Carpentaria
INDIAN OCEAN
Great Barrier Reef
Cairns
Townsville
Mackay
NORTHERN TERRITORY
QUEENSLAND
Great Dividing
Great Sandy Desert
Dampier
AUSTRALIA
Alice Springs
Ayers Rock
WESTERN AUSTRALIA
Lake Eyre Basin
L. Eyre
Great Victoria Desert
SOUTH AUSTRALIA
Darling
NEW SOUTH WALES
Geraldton
Kalgoorlie
Sydney
Wollongong
Murray
Perth
Fremantle
Great Australian Bight
Adelaide
Canberra
VICTORIA
Melbourne
Geelong
Bass Strait
Hobart
TASMANIA
110
120
130
140
150
10
20
30
40
A
B
C
D
1
2
3
4
5

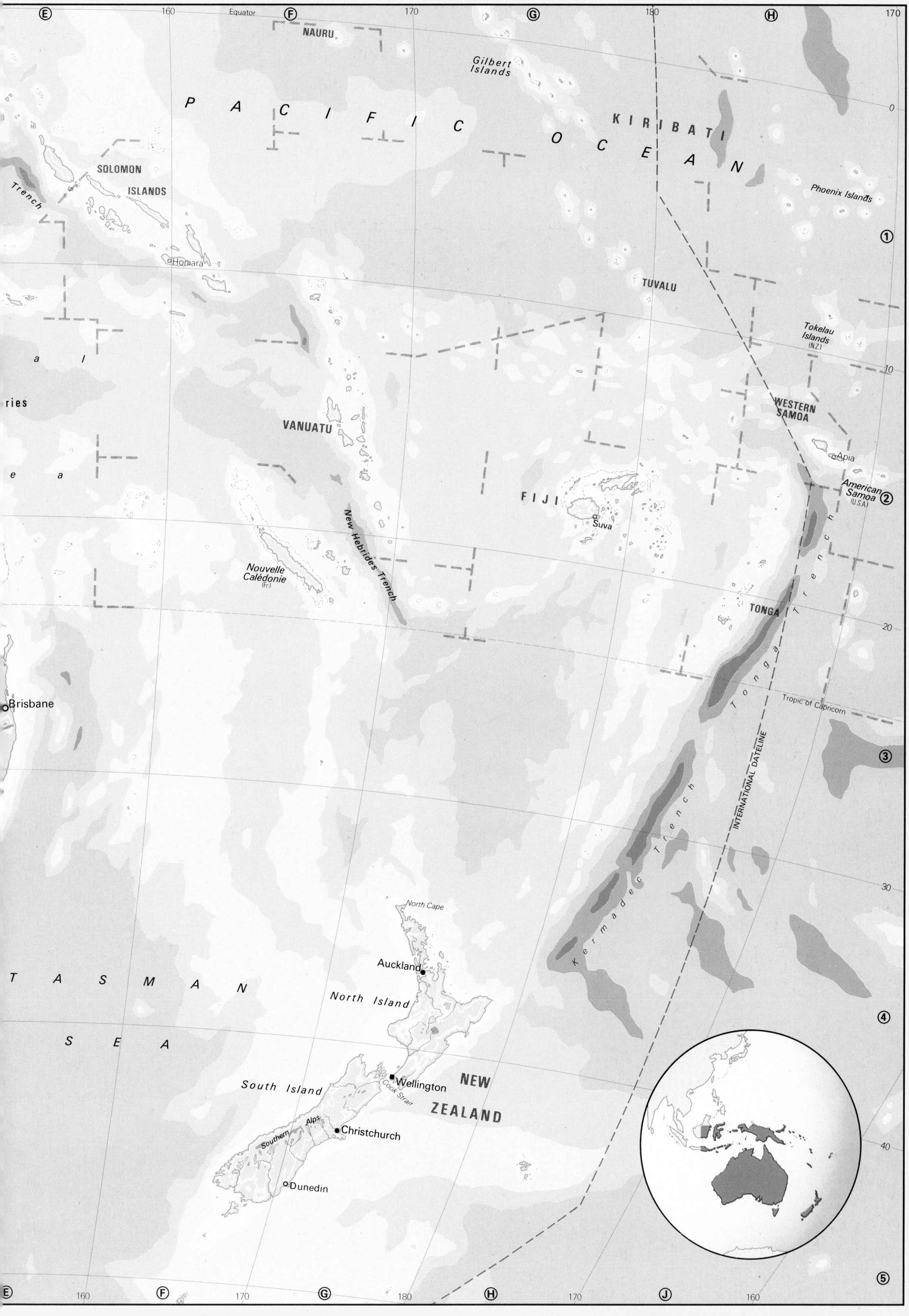
PACIFIC OCEAN
NAURU
Gilbert Islands
KIRIBATI
Phoenix Islands
SOLOMON ISLANDS
Honiara
TUVALU
Tokelau Islands (N.Z.)
WESTERN SAMOA
Apia
American Samoa (U.S.A.)
VANUATU
FIJI
Suva
New Hebrides Trench
Nouvelle Calédonie (Fr.)
TONGA
Tonga Trench
Tropic of Capricorn
INTERNATIONAL DATELINE
Kermadec Trench
Brisbane
North Cape
Auckland
North Island
TASMAN SEA
NEW ZEALAND
Wellington
Cook Strait
South Island
Southern Alps
Christchurch
Dunedin
Equator
160
170
180
170
160
0
10
20
30
40
E
F
G
H
J
1
2
3
4
5

1:5M

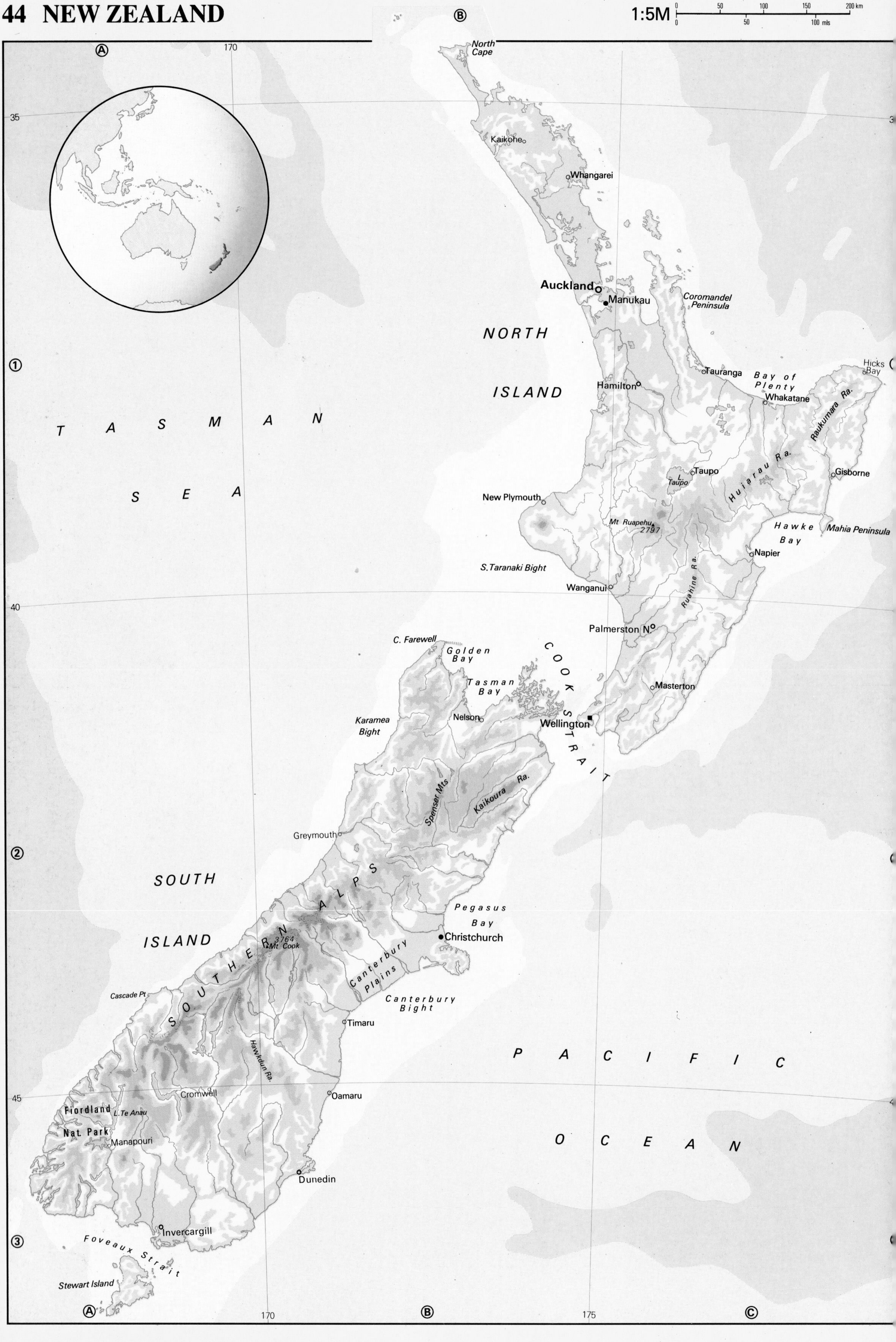
0 50 100 150 200 km
0 50 100 mls
North Cape
Kaikohe
Whangarei
Auckland
Manukau
Coromandel Peninsula
NORTH
ISLAND
Hamilton
Tauranga
Bay of Plenty
Whakatane
Hicks Bay
Raukumara Ra.
Huiarau Ra.
Taupo
L. Taupo
Gisborne
New Plymouth
Mt Ruapehu 2797
Hawke Bay
Mahia Peninsula
Napier
S. Taranaki Bight
Ruahine Ra.
Wanganui
Palmerston N.
T A S M A N
S E A
C. Farewell
Golden Bay
Tasman Bay
COOK STRAIT
Masterton
Karamea Bight
Nelson
Wellington
Spenser Mts
Kaikoura Ra.
Greymouth
SOUTH
ISLAND
SOUTHERN ALPS
Pegasus Bay
Christchurch
3764 Mt. Cook
Canterbury Plains
Canterbury Bight
Cascade Pt
Timaru
Hawkdun Ra.
P A C I F I C
O C E A N
Cromwell
Oamaru
Fiordland Nat. Park
L. Te Anau
Manapouri
Dunedin
Invercargill
Foveaux Strait
Stewart Island
35
40
45
170
175
A
B
C
1
2
3

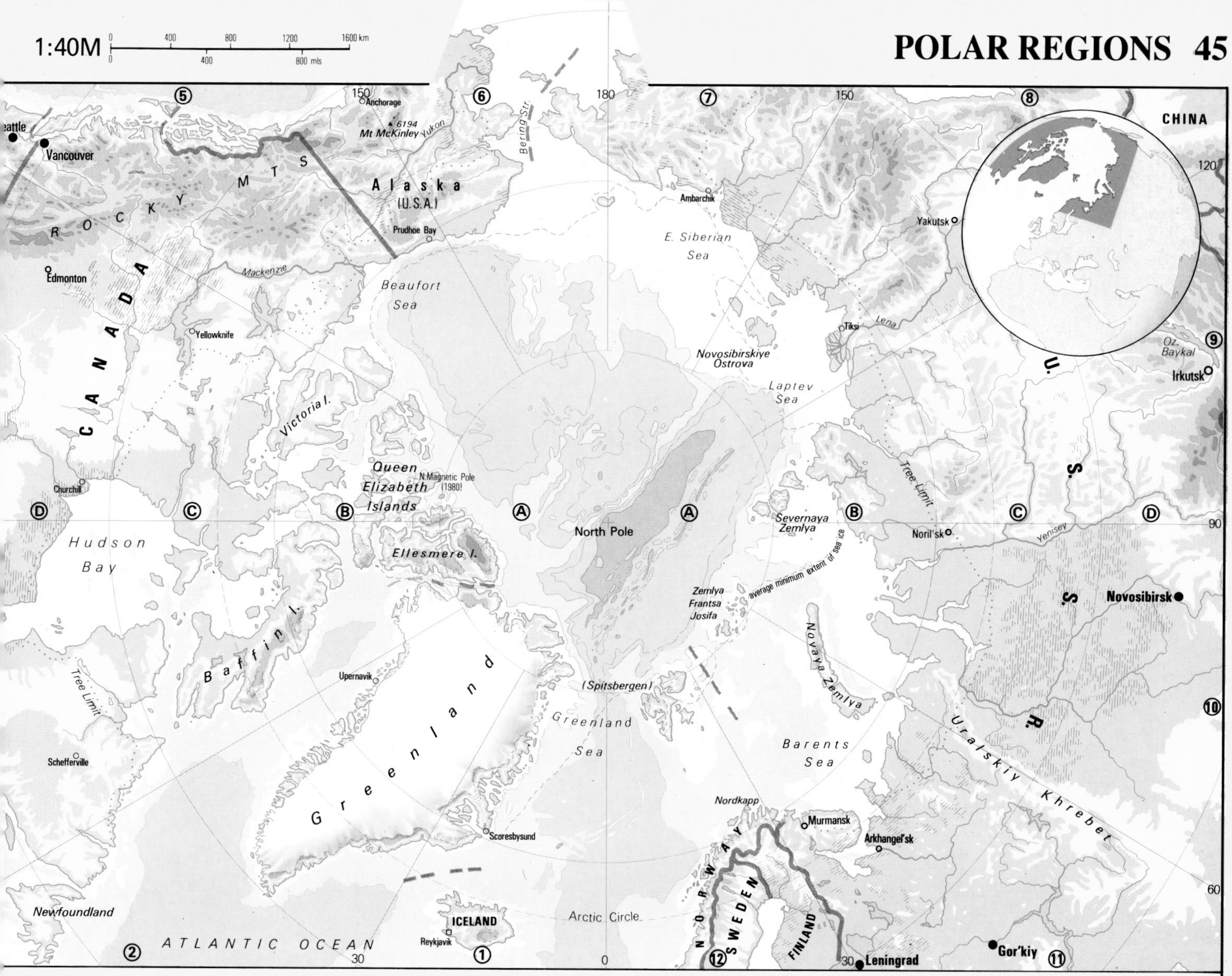
Seattle
Vancouver
Anchorage
6194 Mt McKinley
Yukon
Bering Str.
Alaska (U.S.A.)
Prudhoe Bay
ROCKY MTS
CANADA
Edmonton
Mackenzie
Yellowknife
Beaufort Sea
Ambarchik
E. Siberian Sea
Yakutsk
CHINA
Tiksi
Lena
Novosibirskiye Ostrova
Laptev Sea
Oz. Baykal
Irkutsk
U. S. S. R.
Victoria I.
Queen Elizabeth Islands
N.Magnetic Pole (1980)
Churchill
Hudson Bay
Ellesmere I.
North Pole
Severnaya Zemlya
Noril'sk
Yenisey
Tree Limit
Novosibirsk
Zemlya Frantsa Josifa
average minimum extent of sea ice
Baffin I.
Upernavik
Greenland
(Spitsbergen)
Greenland Sea
Novaya Zemlya
Barents Sea
Uralskiy Khrebet
Schefferville
Nordkapp
Murmansk
Arkhangel'sk
Scoresbysund
NORWAY
SWEDEN
FINLAND
Newfoundland
ICELAND
Reykjavik
Arctic Circle
ATLANTIC OCEAN
Leningrad
Gor'kiy
150 180 150 120 90 60 30 0 30

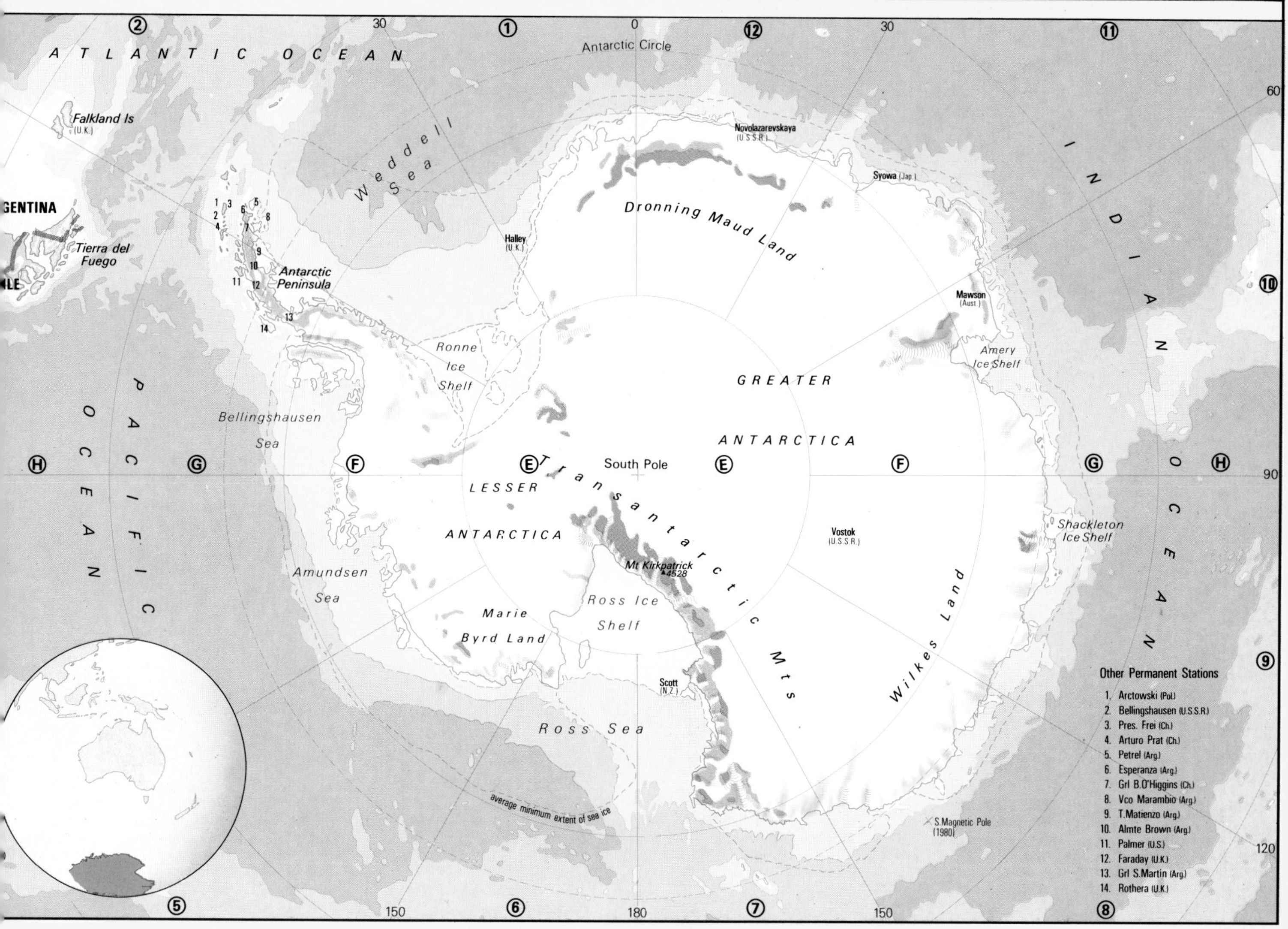
ATLANTIC OCEAN
Antarctic Circle
Falkland Is (U.K.)
Novolazarevskaya (U.S.S.R.)
Syowa (Jap.)
Weddell Sea
ARGENTINA
Tierra del Fuego
CHILE
Halley (U.K.)
Dronning Maud Land
INDIAN OCEAN
Antarctic Peninsula
Mawson (Aust.)
Ronne Ice Shelf
Amery Ice Shelf
GREATER ANTARCTICA
PACIFIC OCEAN
Bellingshausen Sea
South Pole
LESSER ANTARCTICA
Transantarctic Mts
Vostok (U.S.S.R.)
Shackleton Ice Shelf
Amundsen Sea
Mt Kirkpatrick 4528
Ross Ice Shelf
Marie Byrd Land
Wilkes Land
Scott (N.Z.)
Ross Sea
average minimum extent of sea ice
S.Magnetic Pole (1980)
Other Permanent Stations
1. Arctowski (Pol.)
2. Bellingshausen (U.S.S.R.)
3. Pres. Frei (Ch.)
4. Arturo Prat (Ch.)
5. Petrel (Arg.)
6. Esperanza (Arg.)
7. Grl B.O'Higgins (Ch.)
8. Vco Marambio (Arg.)
9. T.Matienzo (Arg.)
10. Almte Brown (Arg.)
11. Palmer (U.S.)
12. Faraday (U.K.)
13. Grl S.Martin (Arg.)
14. Rothera (U.K.)
30 0 30 60 90 120 150 180 150

1:35M

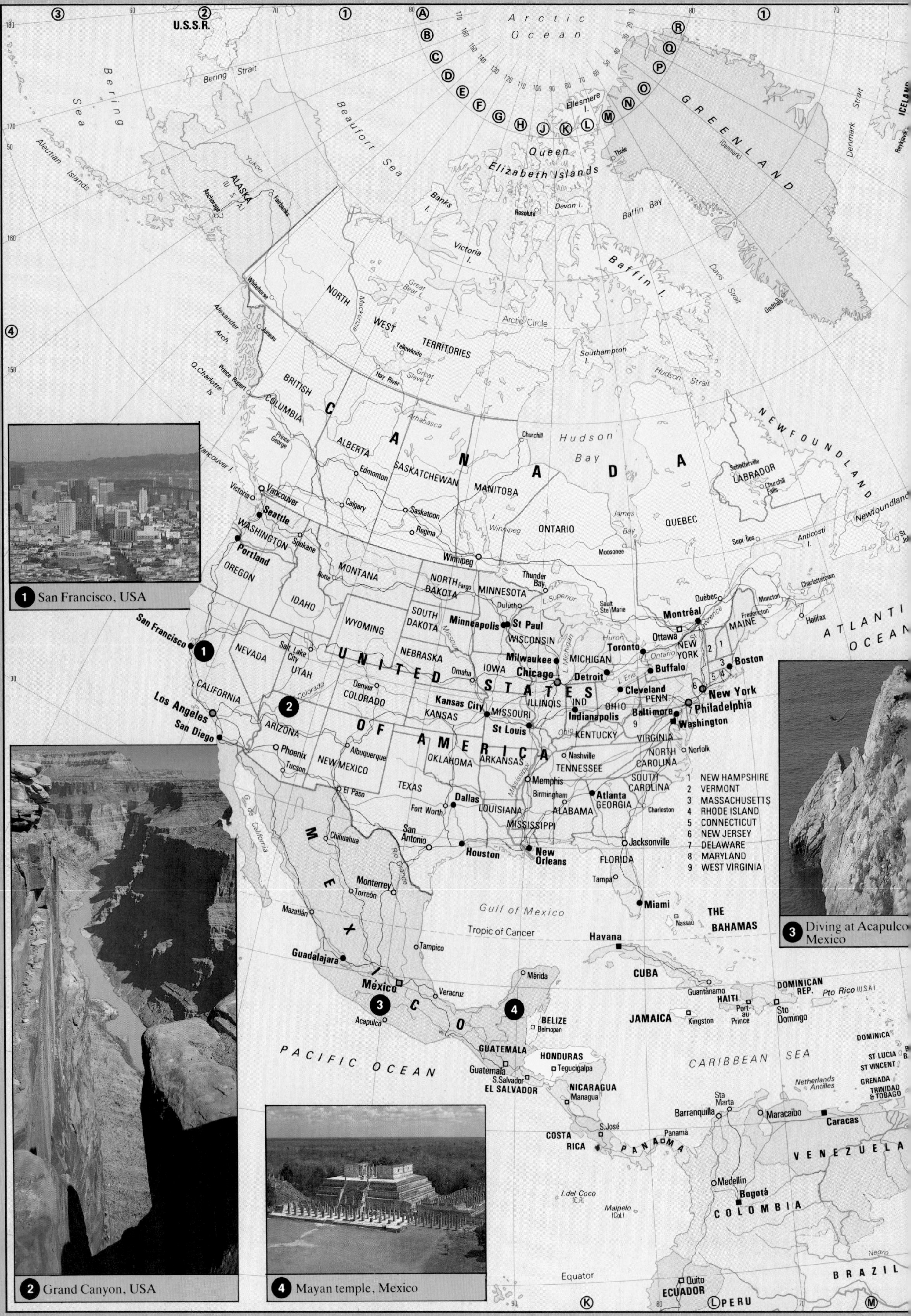

1 San Francisco, USA

2 Grand Canyon, USA

4 Mayan temple, Mexico

3 Diving at Acapulco, Mexico

DID YOU KNOW THAT …?

1 The city of San Francisco was almost destroyed by an earthquake in 1906, and there could be another one soon! Right under the city runs the San Andreas fault, where two of the 'plates' which make up the earth's crust slide against one another. When they get jammed together at any point, pressure builds up, until finally they break apart. This causes an earthquake because of the sudden release of so much energy. The longer the plates stay jammed together, the greater the strength of the final earthquake: in 1906, the plates under San Francisco slid 6 m (20 feet) in a few minutes! Some parts of the fault have not moved for years – and scientists think there will be another big earthquake soon.

2 The huge Grand Canyon in Arizona, USA, was gouged out of the rock by the Colorado River. It is 1.6 km (1 mile) deep, a maximum of 29 km (18 miles) wide and no less than 446 km (227 miles) long! The Grand Canyon is still being carved deeper (though very slowly) by the river.

3 At La Questrada, Acapulco, Mexico, divers often swoop 36 m (118 feet) down into the sea! This is the highest dive which people do regularly.

4 The Maya were a tribe who lived in southern Mexico and Guatemala 1400 years ago. They built great cities with stone temples, public buildings and palaces. The picture shows one of their buildings which can be seen today. It was built without help from any modern machinery!

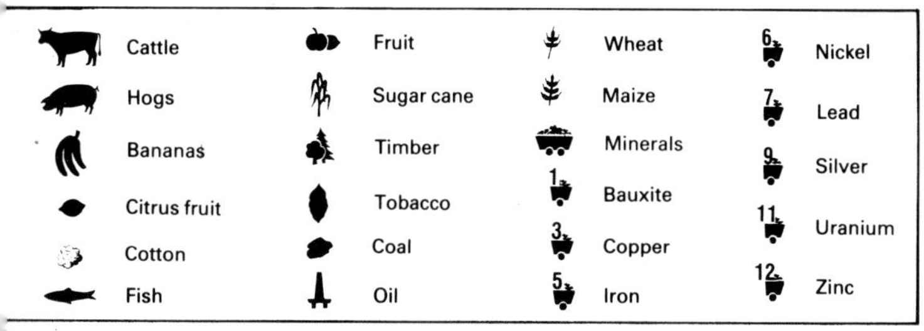

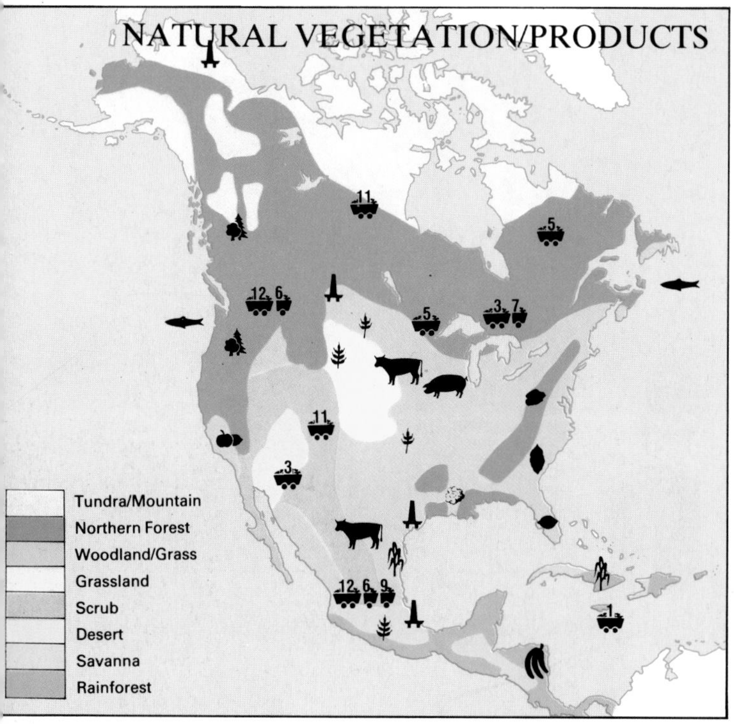

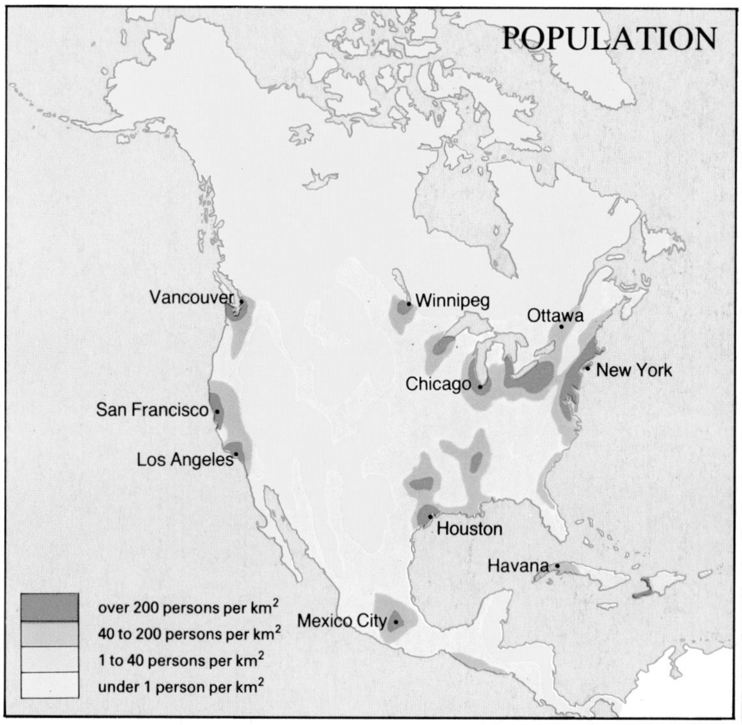

CANADA

Area: 9 976 147 sq km (3 851 790 sq miles)
Population: 25 100 000
Capital: Ottawa
Languages: English, French
Currency: Canadian Dollar

CUBA

Area: 114 524 sq km (44 218 sq miles)
Population: 9 900 000
Capital: Havana
Language: Spanish
Currency: Cuban Peso

EL SALVADOR

Area: 20 865 sq km (8056 sq miles)
Population: 4 800 000
Capital: San Salvador
Language: Spanish
Currency: Colon

GUATEMALA

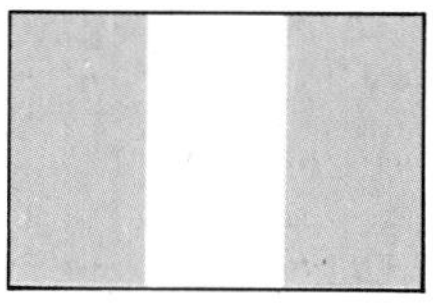

Area: 108 888 sq km (42 042 sq miles)
Population: 8 000 000
Capital: Guatemala
Language: Spanish
Currency: Quetzal

JAMAICA

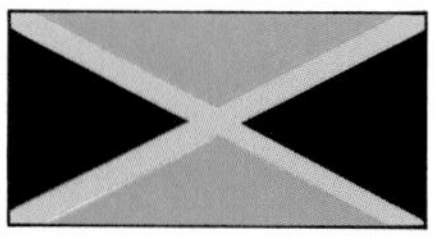

Area: 11 424 sq km (4411 sq miles)
Population: 2 400 000
Capital: Kingston
Language: English
Currency: Jamaican Dollar

MEXICO

Area: 1 967 180 sq km (759 528 sq miles)
Population: 77 000 000
Capital: Mexico City
Language: Spanish
Currency: Mexican Peso

NICARAGUA

Area: 139 000 sq km (53 668 sq miles)
Population: 2 900 000
Capital: Managua
Language: Spanish
Currency: Cordoba

UNITED STATES OF AMERICA

Area: 9 363 130 sq km (3 615 104 sq miles)
Population: 236 300 000
Capital: Washington
Language: English
Currency: U.S. Dollar

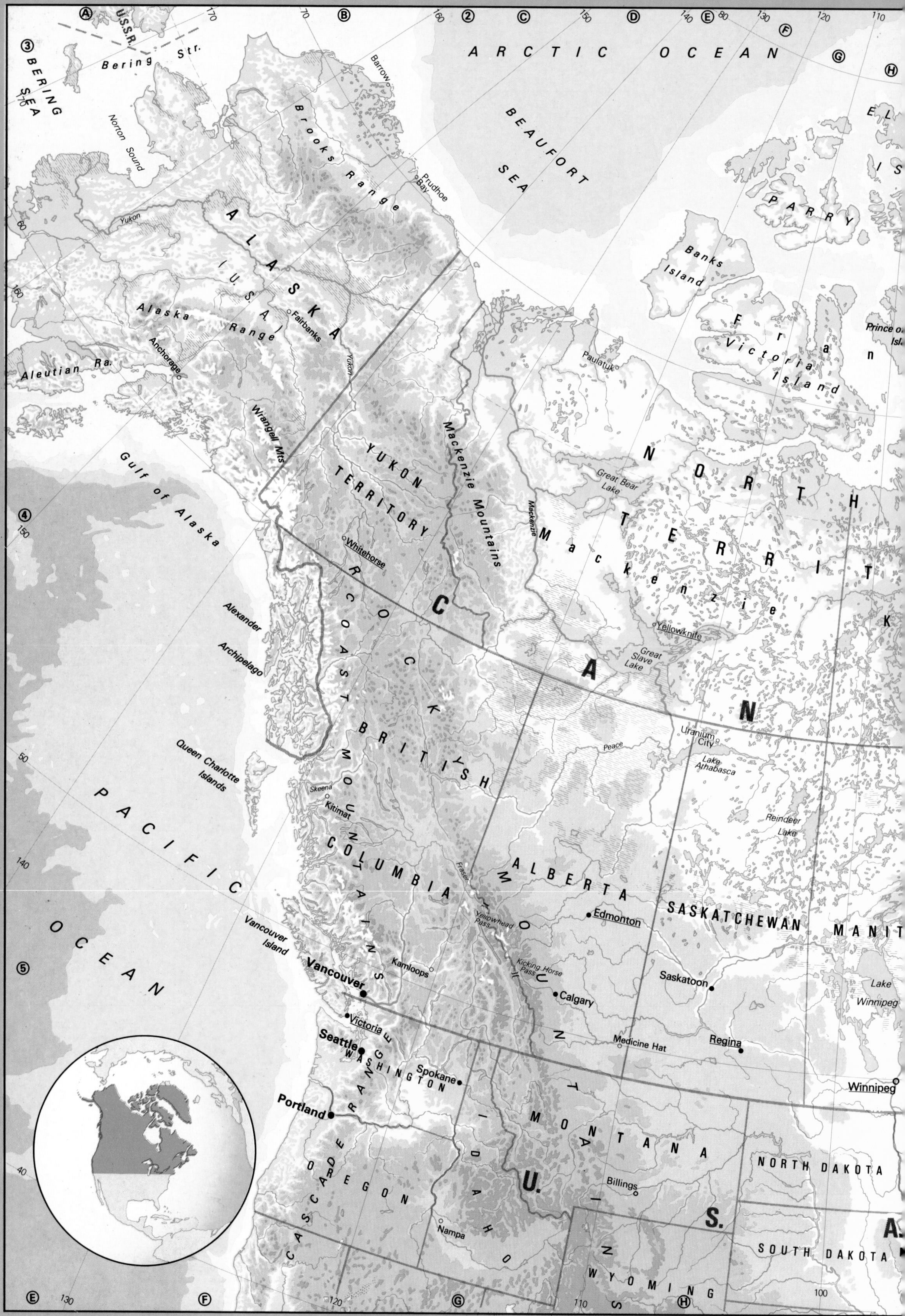
ARCTIC OCEAN
BEAUFORT SEA
BERING SEA
Bering Str.
U.S.S.R.
Norton Sound
Barrow
Prudhoe Bay
Brooks Range
ALASKA (U.S.A.)
Alaska Range
Fairbanks
Anchorage
Aleutian Ra.
Yukon
Wrangell Mts
Gulf of Alaska
YUKON TERRITORY
Whitehorse
Mackenzie Mountains
Mackenzie
Banks Island
Victoria Island
PARRY
Prince of ... Island
Paulatuk
Great Bear Lake
NORTHWEST TERRITORIES
Yellowknife
Great Slave Lake
CANADA
Uranium City
Lake Athabasca
Reindeer Lake
Peace
ROCKY MOUNTAINS
COAST MOUNTAINS
BRITISH COLUMBIA
Alexander Archipelago
Queen Charlotte Islands
Skeena
Kitimat
Fraser
Yellowhead Pass
Kicking Horse Pass
ALBERTA
Edmonton
Calgary
SASKATCHEWAN
Saskatoon
Regina
Medicine Hat
MANITOBA
Lake Winnipeg
Winnipeg
PACIFIC OCEAN
Vancouver Island
Vancouver
Kamloops
Victoria
Seattle
WASHINGTON
Spokane
Portland
CASCADE RANGE
OREGON
IDAHO
Nampa
MONTANA
Billings
WYOMING
NORTH DAKOTA
SOUTH DAKOTA
U.S.A.
Mackenzie
0 100 200 300 mls

GREENLAND
ICELAND
Reykjavik
DENMARK STRAIT
Etah
Dundas
Kraulshavn
BAFFIN BAY
Christianshab
Angmagssalik
Arctic Circle
Baffin Island
Clyde
DAVIS STRAIT
Kekertuk
Qagssimiut
Foxe Basin
Cumberland Sound
Cape Dorset
HUDSON STRAIT
Labrador Sea
NEWFOUNDLAND
Ungava Bay
Smith I.
Povungnituk
HUDSON BAY
Churchill
Cartwright
Labrador
Schefferville
Newfoundland
St John's
Fort Severn
Labrador City
QUEBEC
Sept-Iles
Gulf of Saint Lawrence
Attawapiskat
Ft Rupert
Chibougamau
St Lawrence
PRINCE EDWARD I.
NEW BRUNSWICK
NOVA SCOTIA
ONTARIO
Québec
Halifax
Noranda
MAINE
Thunder Bay
LAKE SUPERIOR
ATLANTIC OCEAN
Montréal
St Lawrence Seaway
Duluth
Sudbury
Ottawa
VERMONT
NEW HAMPSHIRE
MICHIGAN
L. HURON
St Paul
L. MICHIGAN
Toronto
L. Ontario
MASS.
Boston
Providence
WISCONSIN
Hamilton
Rochester
NEW YORK
Kitchener
Buffalo
Hartford
CONN.
Madison
Milwaukee
Detroit
L. Erie

1:12.5M

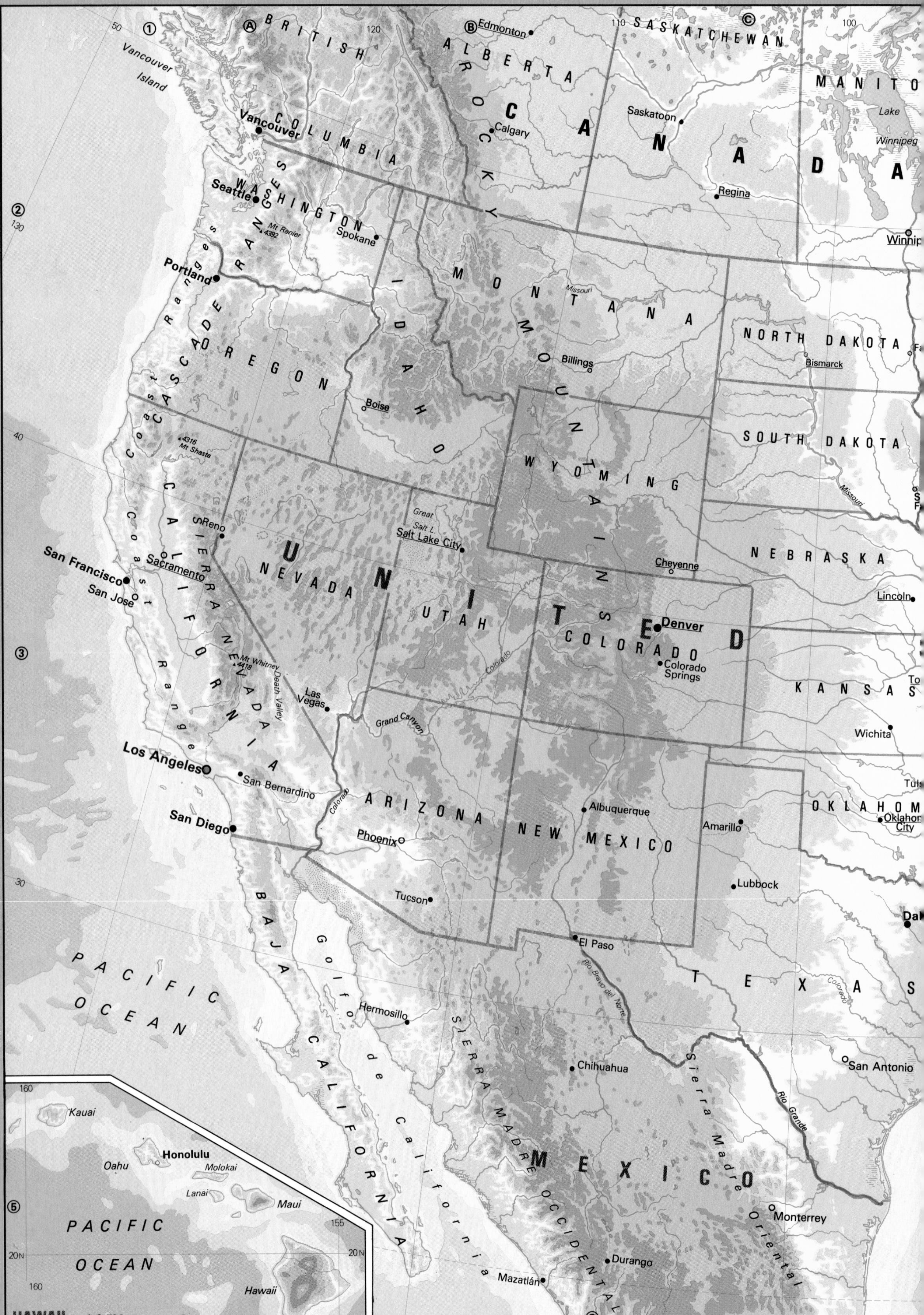

① ② ③

Ⓐ Ⓑ Ⓒ

BRITISH COLUMBIA
Vancouver Island
Vancouver
Seattle
Mt Ranier 4392
Spokane
Portland
WASHINGTON
CASCADE RANGES
OREGON
Mt Shasta 4316
C A N A D A
ALBERTA
Edmonton
Calgary
SASKATCHEWAN
Saskatoon
Regina
MANITO
Lake Winnipeg
Winnip

ROCKY MOUNTAINS
IDAHO
Boise
MONTANA
Billings
Missouri
NORTH DAKOTA
Bismarck
Fa

WYOMING
SOUTH DAKOTA
Missouri
SF

Reno
NEVADA
Great Salt L.
Salt Lake City
UTAH
U N I T E D
Cheyenne
NEBRASKA
Lincoln
To

San Francisco
Sacramento
San Jose
CALIFORNIA
SIERRA NEVADA
Mt Whitney 4418
Death Valley
Las Vegas
Colorado
Denver
COLORADO
Colorado Springs
S
K A N S A S
Wichita
Tu

Los Angeles
San Bernardino
San Diego
Coast Ranges
Grand Canyon
Colorado
ARIZONA
Phoenix
Tucson
NEW MEXICO
Albuquerque
Amarillo
Lubbock
El Paso
OKLAHOM
Oklahoma City
Da

PACIFIC OCEAN
BAJA CALIFORNIA
Golfo de California
Hermosillo
SIERRA MADRE OCCIDENTAL
Rio Bravo del Norte
Chihuahua
T E X A S
Colorado
San Antonio
Rio Grande
M E X I C O
Durango
Mazatlán
SIERRA MADRE ORIENTAL
Monterrey

HAWAII 1:6.5M
Ⓗ
Kauai
Oahu
Honolulu
Molokai
Lanai
Maui
Hawaii
PACIFIC OCEAN
⑤
160 155
20N 20 N
100 110
Ⓒ

USSR
Bering Strait
Yukon
Fairbanks
ALASKA
CANADA
Anchorage
Whitehorse
Bering Sea
Gulf of Alaska
Juneau
ALEUTIAN ISLANDS
1:35M
ALASKA
Gulf of Saint Lawrence
St Lawrence
PRINCE EDWARD I.
NEW BRUNSWICK
NOVA SCOTIA
Québec
Fredericton
Saint John
Halifax
QUEBEC
MAINE
Augusta
Thunder Bay
LAKE SUPERIOR
Duluth
MICHIGAN
Sudbury
North Bay
Montréal
Ottawa
St Lawrence Seaway
Montpelier
VERMONT
NEW HAMPSHIRE
Concord
LAKE HURON
ONTARIO
L. MICHIGAN
St Paul
Minneapolis
Mississippi
WISCONSIN
Toronto
L. ONTARIO
Niagara Falls
Albany
MASS.
Boston
Providence
R.I.
Hartford
CONN.
Buffalo
NEW YORK
LAKE ERIE
Milwaukee
Detroit
Cleveland
Toledo
Newark
New York
N.J.
Philadelphia
Chicago
IOWA
PENNSYLVANIA
INDIANA
OHIO
Pittsburgh
Columbus
MD
Dover
Annapolis
Baltimore
Washington D.C.
DEL.
ILLINOIS
UNITED STATES
APPALACHIAN MOUNTAINS
Indianapolis
Cincinnati
Ohio
WEST VIRGINIA
Charleston
Kansas City
Missouri
St Louis
Louisville
Lexington
VIRGINIA
Richmond
MISSOURI
KENTUCKY
Ozark Plateaus
Raleigh
NORTH CAROLINA
Nashville
TENNESSEE
ATLANTIC OCEAN
Memphis
SOUTH CAROLINA
Columbia
Little Rock
Atlanta
ARKANSAS
Birmingham
ALABAMA
GEORGIA
MISSISSIPPI
Jackson
Jacksonville
FLORIDA
Tallahassee
LOUISIANA
Baton Rouge
New Orleans
Houston
Tampa
Lake Okeechobee
THE BAHAMAS
Miami
Nassau
Tropic of Cancer
GULF OF MEXICO
Straits of Florida
Andros
Havana (Habana)
CUBA

UNITED STATES
CALIFORNIA
ARIZONA
NEW MEXICO
OKLAHOMA
TEXAS
ARKANSAS
TENNESSEE
LOUISIANA
MISSISSIPPI
ALABAMA
GEORGIA
SOUTH CAROLINA
NORTH CAROLINA
FLORIDA
San Diego
Mexicali
Phoenix
Tucson
Albuquerque
Amarillo
Dallas
Houston
San Antonio
Memphis
Baton Rouge
New Orleans
Birmingham
Atlanta
Columbus
Columbia
Jacksonville
Tampa
Miami
Colorado
Mississippi
Rio Bravo del Norte
Rio Grande
Cd Juárez
Hermosillo
Ciudad Obregón
Chihuahua
Culiacán
Nuevo Laredo
Monterrey
Guadalupe
Matamoros
Tampico
Guadalajara
León
México
Popocatepetl
5452
Citlaltepetl
5699
Puebla
Veracruz
Oaxaca
Acapulco
Tehuantepec
Istmo de Tehuantepec
Villahermosa
Mérida
Yucatan
MEXICO
Sierra Madre Occidental
Sierra Madre Oriental
Baja California
Golfo de California
C. Falso
Tropic of Cancer
GULF OF MEXICO
Bahía de Campeche
Yucatan Channel
Straits of Florida
Great Bahama Bank
THE BAHAMAS
Nassau
Andros
Havana (Habana)
Sta Clara
CUBA
Guantánamo
JAMAICA
Kingston
CARIBBEAN SEA
PACIFIC OCEAN
BELIZE
Belmopan
GUATEMALA
Guatemala
Tapachula
EL SALVADOR
San Salvador
HONDURAS
S. Pedro Sula
Tegucigalpa
NICARAGUA
Managua
COSTA RICA
San José
PANAMA
Panama
30
20
10
110
100
90
80
A
B
C
D
E
1
2
3
4
0
100
200
300 mls

1:10M 0 100 200 300 400 km
0 100 200 mls

ATLANTIC OCEAN
CARIBBEAN SEA
GREATER ANTILLES
LESSER ANTILLES
Leeward Islands
Windward Islands
PUERTO RICO TRENCH
CAYMAN TRENCH
THE BAHAMAS
CUBA
Havana (Habana)
Pinar del Río
Santa Clara
Sagua la Grande
Camagüey
Holguín
Santiago de Cuba
Guantánamo
Miami
FLORIDA
Straits of Florida
Tropic of Cancer
Great Abaco
Eleuthera
Nassau
Andros
Acklins
Great Inagua
Caicos Is (U.K.)
Cayman Islands (U.K.)
JAMAICA
Kingston
Montego Bay
Hispaniola
HAITI
Port-au-Prince
Port-de-Paix
Jacmel
Cordillera Central
DOMINICAN REPUBLIC
Santo Domingo
Santiago
La Romana
PUERTO RICO (U.S.A.)
San Juan
Caguas
Ponce
Aguadilla
Virgin Is (U.S.A. & U.K.)
ST KITTS-NEVIS
ANTIGUA & BARBUDA
Guadeloupe (Fr.)
Basse Terre
DOMINICA
Roseau
Martinique (Fr.)
ST LUCIA
Castries
ST VINCENT
Kingstown
GRENADA
St George's
BARBADOS
Bridgetown
TRINIDAD AND TOBAGO
Tobago
Trinidad
Port of Spain
VENEZUELA
Caracas
Valencia
Barquisimeto
Maracaibo
Cabimas
Lago de Maracaibo
G. de Venezuela
Carúpano
Maturín
Cd Guayana
COLOMBIA
Barranquilla
Cartagena
Ciénaga
Valledupar
Montería
Golfo del Darién
PANAMA
Panamá
Panama Canal
COSTA RICA
San José
NICARAGUA
Prinzapolca
HONDURAS
Caratasca
JAMAICA 1:25M
Montego Bay
Savanna la Mar
Mandeville
Chapeltown
St Ann's Bay
Kingston
Blue Mts
Pt Antonio
Portland Pt
TRINIDAD 1:25M
Pt of Spain
Arima
St Joseph
San Fernando
Gulf of Paria
Fullarton
Crown Pt
Moriah
GRENADA 1:25M
Sauteurs
St George's
ST VINCENT 1:25M
Georgetown
Kingstown
ST LUCIA 1:25M
Castries
Vieux Fort
DOMINICA 1:25M
Marigot
Roseau
BARBADOS 1:25M
Speightstown
Bridgetown

1:35M

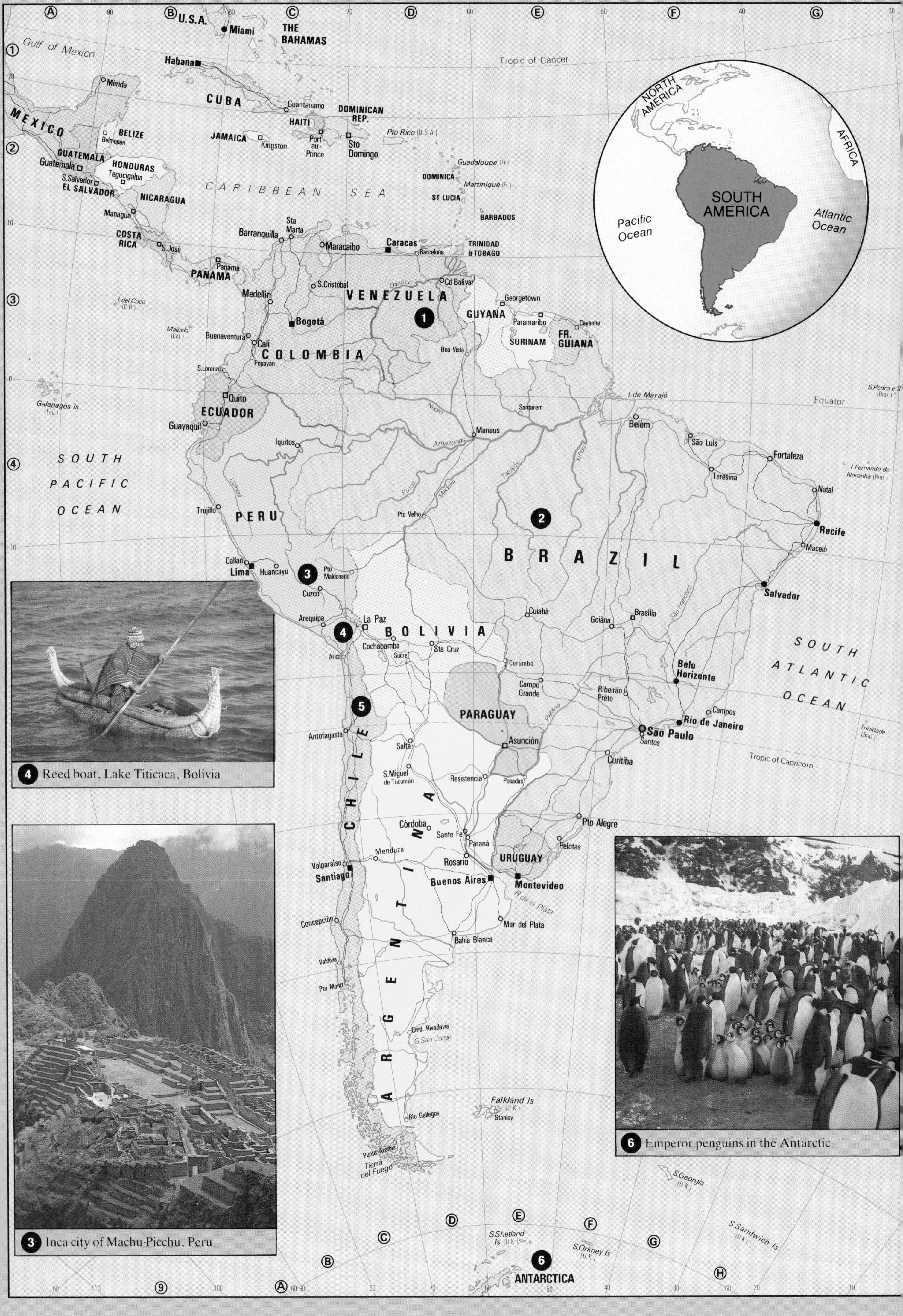

4 Reed boat, Lake Titicaca, Bolivia

3 Inca city of Machu-Picchu, Peru

6 Emperor penguins in the Antarctic

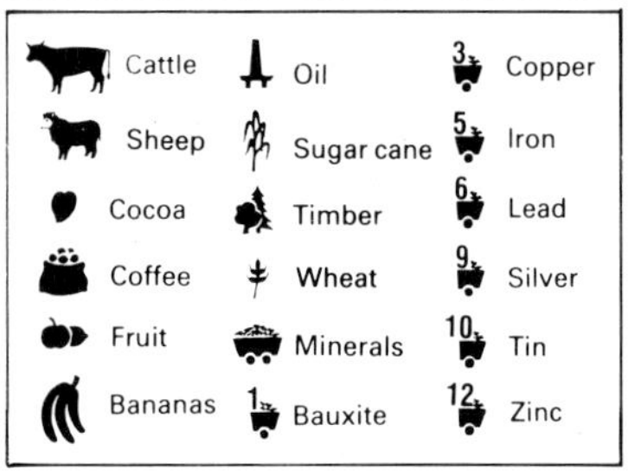

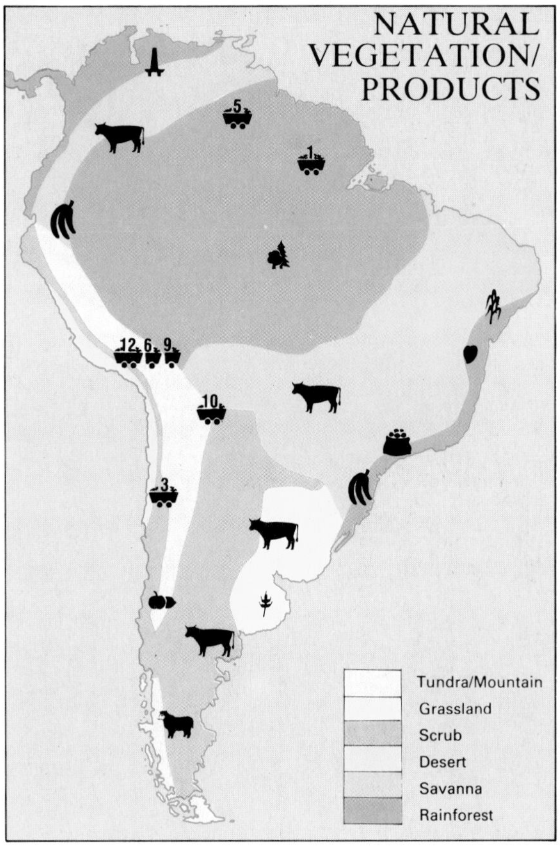

DID YOU KNOW THAT ...?

1 The Angel Falls, Venezuela, are the highest waterfalls in the world, at 979 m (3212 feet).

2 Deforestation is a major problem in South America. About 1 per cent of the total area of forest is lost each year! Often trees are cut down to clear land for agriculture. On hillsides, the soil soon becomes too poor to grow crops and the land is abandoned. Trees cannot grow again, and so soil is eroded away by rain and wind. Trees are also lost when lakes are made for hydro-electric dams; when new towns are built; and as a result of the way people live – they take too much wood for fuel and timber, allow animals to graze on foliage, and light fires which get out of control.

3 In the Andes Mountains, in the north-west of South America, there are ruins of cities built by the Incas. They ruled the Indians in the area 500 years ago. The Incas had well-developed political and religious systems. They built their cities on terraces engineered from the mountain side. The Spanish, the first Europeans to discover these cities, killed the Incas to seize the gold and silver which they had mined, and their cities were abandoned.

4 The highest navigable lake in the world is Lake Titicaca, on the Peru/Bolivia border. It is no less than 3811 m (12 503 feet) above sea level! The local Indian people make boats from bundles of reeds tied together, to use for fishing. The reeds grow around the edge of the lake.

5 Although in the rain forests of the Amazon Basin it rains every day, in the Atacama Desert, Chile, hundreds of years can pass between one rain storm and the next! A storm in 1971 was the first for 400 years. The desert is the driest place in the world.

6 The Emperor Penguin, found in the Antarctic, does not make a nest. Instead, a single egg is carried on top of the male penguin's feet! It is kept warm by a fold of skin which hangs down and covers it. The penguin does not eat during the two months it takes for the egg to hatch out!

ARGENTINA

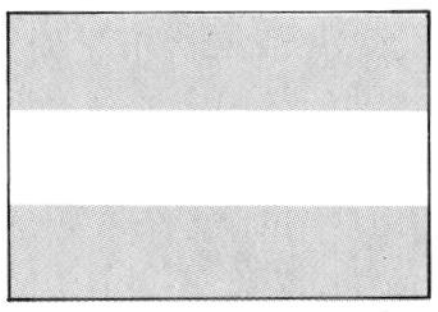

Area: 2 777 815 sq km (1 072 514 sq miles)
Population: 29 100 000
Capital: Buenos Aires
Language: Spanish
Currency: Argentine Peso

BOLIVIA

Area: 1 098 575 sq km (424 160 sq miles)
Population: 6 000 000
Capital: La Paz
Languages: Spanish, Aymara, Quechua
Currency: Bolivian Peso

BRAZIL

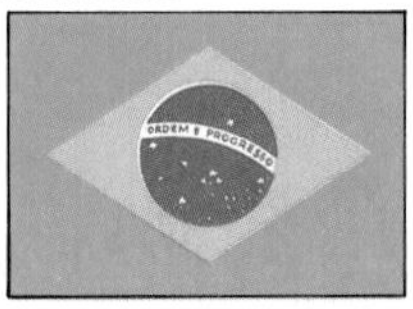

Area: 8 511 968 sq km (3 286 471 sq miles)
Population: 134 400 000
Capital: Brasilia
Language: Portuguese
Currency: Cruzeiro

CHILE

Area: 756 943 sq km (292 256 sq miles)
Population: 11 900 000
Capital: Santiago
Language: Spanish
Currency: Chilean Peso

COLOMBIA

Area: 1 138 907 sq km (439 732 sq miles)
Population: 28 200 000
Capital: Bogota
Language: Spanish
Currency: Colombian Peso

ECUADOR

Area: 455 502 sq km (175 869 sq miles)
Population: 9 100 000
Capital: Quito
Language: Spanish
Currency: Sucre

GUYANA

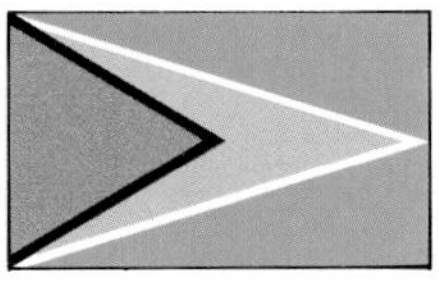

Area: 214 969 sq km (83 000 sq miles)
Population: 800 000
Capital: Georgetown
Language: English
Currency: Guyanese Dollar

PERU

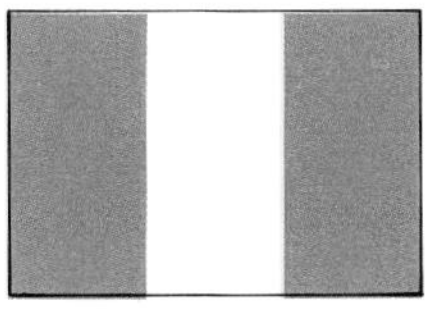

Area: 1 285 215 sq km (496 222 sq miles)
Population: 19 200 000
Capital: Lima
Languages: Spanish, Aymara, Quechua
Currency: Sol

VENEZUELA

Area: 912 047 sq km (352 141 sq miles)
Population: 18 600 000
Capital: Caracas
Language: Spanish
Currency: Bolivar

1:15M

Roseau
Martinique
ST LUCIA
Castries
ST VINCENT
Kingstown
GRENADA
St George's
Port of Spain
Tegucigalpa
NICARAGUA
Managua
San José
COSTA RICA
Panama
PANAMA
Neth. Antilles
Curaçao
(Neth.)
Sta Marta
Barranquilla
Valledupar
Maracaibo
Cabimas
Caracas
Valencia
Maracay
Barquisimeto
Monteria
Cúcuta
San Cristóbal
Bucaramanga
L L A N O S
VENEZUELA
Orinoco
Cd Guayana
Angel Falls
Cord. Occidental
Cord. Oriental
Cord. Central
Bello
Itagui
Medellín
Manizales
Pereira
Cartago
Armenia
Bogotá
Buenaventura
Palmira
Cali
Neiva
COLOMBIA
Calamar
RORAIMA
Pasto
Icana
Negro
Quito
5896
Cotopaxi
ECUADOR
Chimborazo
6267
Guayaquil
Manacapuru
Iquitos
Amazonas
Tabatinga
AMAZONAS
SELVAS
Piura
Chiclayo
Humaitá
Cruzeiro do Sul
Pucallpa
Trujillo
Chimbote
Pôrto Velho
ACRE
Rio Branco
RONDÔNIA
B
CORDILLERA DE LOS ANDES
PERU
Callao
Lima
Huancayo
Machu Picchu
Cuzco
Trinidad
PACIFIC OCEAN
L. Titicaca
Ancohuma
6388
Arequipa
La Paz
BOLIVIA
Cochabamba
Santa Cruz
Oruro
Arica
Desierto de Atacama
CHILE
Jujuy
Tropic of Capricorn
Antofagasta
ARGENTINA
Salta
at the same scale
GALAPAGOS ISLANDS
(ISLAS GALÁPAGOS)
Isabela
Santa Cruz
Baquerizo Moreno
at the same scale
Islas Juan Fernández
(Chile)
Alejandro Selkirk
Robinson Crusoe
Sta Clara

BARBADOS
Bridgetown
INIDAD AND OBAGO
Mabaruma
Georgetown
Paramaribo
Cayenne
GUYANA
SURINAM
FRENCH GUIANA
ATLANTIC
OCEAN
AMAPÁ
Macapá
Equator
Amazonas
Belém
Santarém
Cametá
naus
São Luís
Monção
Itaituba
PARÁ
Sobral
Fortaleza (Ceará)
MARANHÃO
Imperatriz
Teresina
CEARÁ
Mossoró
RIO GRANDE DO NORTE
Natal
Serra do Cachimbo
Araguaína
PIAUÍ
PARAÍBA
João Pessoa
PERNAMBUCO
Caruaru
Recife (Pernambuco)
São Francisco
BRAZIL
ALAGOAS
Maceió
São Félix
SERGIPE
Aracajú
BAHIA
Barreiras
MATO GROSSO
Feira de S.
Paranã
GOIÁS
Salvador (Bahia)
Planalto de Mato Grosso
Jequié
Vitória da Conquista
Ilhéus
Cáceres
Brasília
Goiânia
Montes Claros
Serra do Espinhaço
Itamaraju
Teófilo Otôni
MATO GROSSO DO SUL
Uberlândia
MINAS GERAIS
Uberaba
ESPÍRITO SANTO
Campo Grande
Belo Horizonte
Caratinga
Colatina
Paraguai
Franca
SÃO PAULO
Cachoeiro
Dourados
Pres. Prudente
Marília
Limeria
Sa de Mantiqueira
Volta Redonda
Nova Friburgo
Londrina
PARAGUAY
Umuarama
Sorocaba
São Paulo
Rio de Janeiro
São Vicente
Asunción
Toledo
PARANÁ
55
50
45
40
35
15
10
5
0
20
G
H
J
K
L
M
1
2
3
4
5
6
7
8

1:15M
0 200 400 600 km
0 100 200 300 mls

This index helps you to find countries and places shown on the maps in this atlas. Each country or place name is listed in alphabetical order (A to Z), letter by letter. For example, Manchester will come after Madagascar and before Melbourne. After each name, extra information in a shortened form may be given. For example, 'Mts' after the entry 'Grampian' means 'mountains'. The list of abbreviations (shortened words) which follows this introduction tells you what each shortened word description means. The next item in each entry is the name of the country in which the place is. Finally there is a reference number which will look something like this: **16C3**. The first number (before the letter) is the page number (here page 16). The letter and second number lead you to the area on the map on that page where the place can be found. Follow the column labelled with the letter shown (here column C) down from the top of the page. Follow the row with the same number (here row 3) in from the side of the page. Where the column and row meet is the part of the map where you will find the place you looked up (**16C3** is the reference for London, England). Practise looking up a few places in the index and on the maps. Try to find Sydney, Australia; New York, U.S.A.; Paris, France.

Arch	Archipelago	O	Ocean
B	Bay	P	Pass
C	Cape	Pass	Passage
Chan	Channel	Pen	Peninsula
Des	Desert	Plat	Plateau
Gl	Glacier	Pt	Point
G. of	Gulf of	Res	Reservoir
H(s)	Hills(s)	R	River
I(s)	Islands(s)	S	Sea
Lg	Lagoon	Sd	Sound
L	Lake	Str	Strait
Mt(s)	Mountain(s)	V	Valley

A

B

C

D

E

F

G

T

U

V

W

X

Y

Z